CHAMBERS

BOOK OF
ARAUCARIA
CROSSWORDS

CHAMBERS

CHAMBERS
An imprint of Chambers Harrap Publishers Ltd
7 Hopetoun Crescent
Edinburgh
EH7 4AY

First published by Chambers Harrap Publishers Ltd 2003

ISBN 0550 10110 1

Project Manager: Una McGovern
Prepress: Alison Auld

Designed and typeset by Chambers Harrap Publishers Ltd, Edinburgh
Printed by Cox & Wyman Ltd, Reading, Berkshire

Foreword
• by Prunella Scales •

'Went too far on boards to avert code being used (9)'

I fell in love with Araucaria years ago: the range of his clues – cricket, English literature embracing Cranmer and the King James Bible, theatre (the solution to the above is 'overacted' in case you didn't get it) – coupled with decidedly left-of-centre politics, and the fact that I could actually solve some of his puzzles, was irresistible.

In one of the published Guardian Crossword books, Araucaria was described as a parson living in Cambridgeshire, and I developed fantasies while on tour at the Cambridge Arts Theatre of meeting him in a country lane and hitting him fairly hard with whatever weapon came to hand. My husband became quite jealous at finding me so frequently in bed with this other man (though severely chaperoned by *Roget's Thesaurus*, *The Chambers Dictionary* and Margaret Drabble's *Companion to English Literature*), but as a fellow crossword freak, he did understand really.

The year before last I sent Araucaria a Christmas card saying something like 'You drive me madder than anyone else in the world I don't know, and I love you', and was intoxicated to receive a card in return, via my agent, saying 'I love you too'.

And it's gone on from there, really. Our children, knowing of my addiction, secretly furnished him with a catalogue of varied and sometimes abstruse biographical material, which helped him compose a crossword for *The Guardian* on the occasion of a recent birthday – I don't want to specify which – so he is now in possession of a good deal of personal information about me.

Where will it all end, wonders confused

Cruel Penal Lass (8,6)

Acknowledgements

This book would never have got off the ground but for Christine Jones, the secretary, publisher and correspondent of *1 Across* for almost twenty years, who has done all the donkeywork as well as doing all that a literary agent would normally do; I owe her a huge debt of gratitude, and if you enjoy the book, so do you!

I am also greatly indebted to Antoinette, the 'Woman in Wiltshire', who has been the checker of my puzzles (including these) for nearly thirty years, and who has saved me from innumerable errors and infelicities. Help and encouragement has come from others too numerous to mention; I thank them all.

Perhaps I should give a special acknowledgement to my employers in my 'day job', the Church of England, for not discouraging me from spending so much of my time in such a trivial pursuit. (I have of course been 'retired' – off and on – for some time now.)

And finally, I am well aware that the whole crossword business depends on the solvers: if you were not prepared to put up with our vagaries, we would be unemployable. So, to those of you who have written kind and/or frank comments, and to those who have suffered in silence, thank you very much, and I hope you will enjoy solving the puzzles in my first book of jigsaw crosswords.

Araucaria

Introduction

I have been making crosswords (of a sort) since the age of nine, helped by parents and teachers, and later inspired by Ximenes of the *Observer*. In the 1950s that paper ran a crossword composing competition, which I won twice. The crossword editor of *The Manchester Guardian* took note of this and invited me to join his team of setters. My first published puzzle appeared in 1958. At some time in the 60s the paper decided we should cease to be anonymous and asked me for a pseudonym; I chose the monkey puzzle tree partly because the word 'monkey' had private resonances, and partly because Desmond Morris had just produced *The Naked Ape*. It was pretty stupid to pick a name which some people can't spell and some can't pronounce (and my choice of pseudonym for the *Financial Times* – Cinephile – isn't much better), but I seem to be stuck with it. I have worked for various other publications, including Oracle Teletext, which was an interesting assignment, and in 1984 I began the publication of what is now called *1 Across*, a monthly magazine containing puzzles of a more varied sort than would be thought suitable in a newspaper, including a bigger range of 'jigsaw crosswords', the type presented in this book.

The problem I was trying to solve then was how to introduce more variety into crosswords without making them more difficult. Fiendishly difficult crosswords will always (as long as they are solvable at all) have a devoted following of the seriously convoluted in mind; but I wanted to keep in touch with the 'ordinary solver' and still do something different. I noticed that many crossword grids were numbered 1–26, so I wondered if I could replace the numbers with letters. In one case it was possible – just – to replace 1,2,3, etc with A,B,C, etc – but that led nowhere: it was much easier to vary the positions of the letters … and so the Alphabetical Jigsaw was born. Solutions each begin with a different letter, and are fitted into the grid jigsaw-wise, wherever they will go. The clues are no more difficult, but the art of the jigsaw is added to the art of the crossword.

My friend the late John Perkin who was crossword editor of *The Guardian* allowed me to experiment with these; he eventually pointed out that they couldn't satisfactorily go on for ever, because there weren't enough words in the language beginning with X or Z. So I looked for other ways of using the jigsaw principle; and having tried putting letters of the alphabet in the unchecked squares, it seemed worth while to write words – then words in sequence – then quotations or aphorisms – and so on. Round the perimeter of a puzzle was the obvious place, hence the Perimetrical Jigsaw (this seemed a suitable name for them). Other types appeared in due course, and had to be given appropriate names – Diametrical, Rhombical, Aphoristical. This last was developed because I wanted to use phrases that didn't have exactly 28 letters (which a Perimetrical requires); so I just wrote them into the grid to start with. The first things I wrote in could be called aphorisms; so I used the name Aphoristical for any puzzle that works along these lines. The names aren't wonderful, but I had to call them something.

Araucaria

Jigsaw Crosswords

All the puzzles in this book are jigsaws and they are grouped into five different types. The rules for each type of jigsaw are printed at the beginning of each section, and are to be applied unless otherwise stated.

There are no numbers in the grids; you have to fit the solutions into the grids jigsaw-wise, wherever they will go. The clues are numbered, for convenience, and they are listed in alphabetical order of their solutions.

ALPHABETICAL JIGSAWS

Solutions begin with the letter indicated. In all the puzzles in this section, the solutions are to be fitted into the diagram jigsaw-wise, wherever they will go; and their clues are listed in alphabetical order of the solutions (except No. 5 which is slightly different).

Jigsaw No. 1 – ALPHABETICAL

Crow's I across is the work of the author of these plays.

A. Enticed the whole upper class to be communists? (7)
B. Fed up with Forbes' fads, perhaps (7,3)
   Prison … but is the groom all right? (9)
C. Herb heard to answer knock? (5)
D. Remove obstruction in river (6)
E. Art deserving of I down in play (7)
F. Red coffee concoction to shove down the throat (5-4)
G. Eucalyptuses aren't good to be up (3,5)
H. See I across
I. (with H) One traffic worker keeping bus moving in play (5,7)
   Bring article into church in consequence (10)
J. Tease a little boy (4)
K. Children's clothing in the dark – wise move (4,4)
L,W,M. She makes you begin to be successful when a climbing aid's around: only was she Fanny in the play? (4,10)
M. See L
   Mixed marriage begins and develops longer (7)
N. Scottish chatter, Beau's gift? (7)
O. Break ice with one log from the Tertiary period (9)
P. I pay out, keeping the king from fever (7)
Q. Directions for living? (8)
R. Small residence with unusual inside treated with sappy product (9)
S. A few – about fifty – following a play (6)
T. Greek character at a distance from China to proscribe fundamentalists (3,7)
U. Largely immoral and distressing of old (5)
V. Form of tinea intervened, and I'm blinded (10)
W. See L
   Deserving people within the pale of no I down in play (5)

Jigsaw No. 1 – ALPHABETICAL

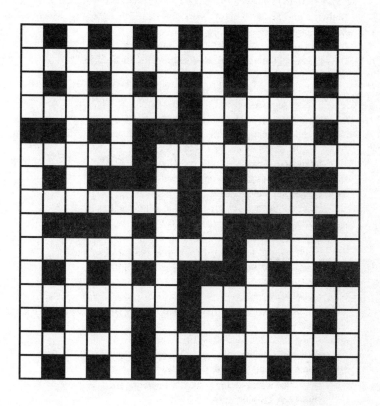

X.   Fox missing half-dozen with marker of territory, having tail almost unprotected (8)

Y.   Every solver's doubtfully loyal about turn (3-3)

Z.   Parsee scriptures last and last (4)

Jigsaw No. 2 – ALPHABETICAL

Once upon a time some authorities included the symbol &, Ampersand, as an extra letter in the alphabet: this puzzle adopts that practice.

- A. Where you are served by the services? (4,1,4,6)
- B. Engagement to speculate on corrupt prince (9)
- C. Quotes about a politician's locations for tents (4,5)
- D& Chancellor with cats in old shop (5,1,4)
- E. Chancellor's old blot on career? (9)
- F. Savage force employed with bills (9)
- G. Drop scone made by Billy boy's Nancy (6-4)
- H. English opening batsmen to find fifth club and so be transferred (5,1,9)
- I. Interested in the West, being pulled along (2,3)
- J. Felicity's sticky fate keeps you to three points (10)
- K. Wagnerian conductor strangely meek about piano (5)
- L. Reddish pigments mostly found in Cumbria (5)
- M. No longer green, coming in from a tureen (6)
- N. Ratios in numbers show investigative quality (8)
  Hurry back to look and see dancer (7)
- O. Rings round electronic device in New Zealand (5)
- P. Fix your eye (if you're Italian) on the wooden puppet (9)
- Q. Some drink nothing – on paper (6)
- R. Go too fast with wrong movement and get covered with marsh plants (4-5)
- S. Actor has Libra on Pisces (6)
- T. Walk up? See next page in link (6)
- U. Coats have unfortunate results (7)
- V. Look at last to sell (4)
- W. Burner in Scotland (4)
- X. Is it cowardly for unknown solver to enter solution? (8)
- Y. A hook may change a Japanese city (8)
- Z. Latin breeze puts his young Roman leaders inside Greek god (8)
- & See D

Jigsaw No. 2 – ALPHABETICAL

Jigsaw No. 3 – ITALIAN ALPHABETICAL

No knowledge of Italian is needed. In normal Italian the letters J, K, W, X and Y are not used; they are not used in this puzzle.

A. Makes steel in glacier, a test of endurance (9)
   High parts of I (4)
B. Best wishes to Doris, the writer surrounded by books (9)
   Right and left of a question? (4,5)
C. More or less antique, well off target (4)
   Prison without having gone too far from home? (7)
D. Died surrounded by churchmen on tennis-court (6)
E. Provide finally with universal English (5)
F. Satisfied before autocrat no. 2 comes in with domestic servant (5,2,7)
G. Insect's characteristic flavour coming back (4)
H. German boy outside takes food (convenience) (9)
   The wrong path home to fix the cover (6)
I. A climber left pub taking a wager on it being used here (7,8)
L. Sleuth the rooster rendered (5)
M. Performed badly, making some din (7)
   Changing houses is pathetic (6)
N. Chemical compound may be revived: ration it (5-10)
O. Letters being sent to far part of Empire? (7)
P. Spenserian poet or (if at pub) Trollope hero, a lewd man by the sound of it (7,8)
Q. Infrequent invocation of Durward (7)
R. Herb to restore the sick: first, an acanthus (7)
S. In the Enterprise's mission it sounds like a bad headache – 5 goes round in it (5,10)
T. Silver ones may be hardest to find if you're young (7)
U. Encourage sawbones to come under the axe (4,2)
V. Jeeves' turn to get currency for a Scot who enjoys ill health (14)
Z. God of the ebbing waterway (4)

Jigsaw No. 3 – ITALIAN ALPHABETICAL

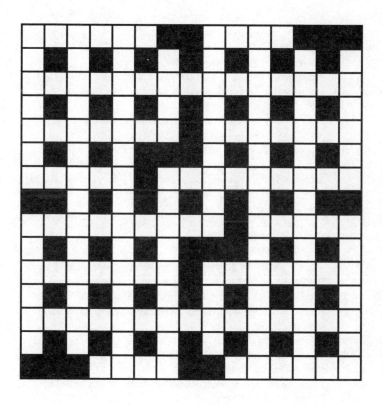

Jigsaw No. 4 – GREEK ALPHABETICAL

No knowledge of Greek is needed.

A. Nobleman with title elevated to Conservative leader: there's a suspicious smell about that (10)

B. The French well placed when put up every two years (8)

G. Ancient physician with a sulphide of lead (6)

D. Associate of Pizarro, a drunkard, in rendering to God (2,4)

E (short). Small landholders or English politicians maybe name two sets (10)

Z. The Channel Islands turn, in a rapid soaring movement, to protection for micro-organisms (10)

E (long). Have a mid-day meal with Alec Hunt? (3,5)

TH. Non-U papers print letter in full and approve imprisoning one drop-out (3,7,5)

I. I hope for the best and I trade one way (8)

K. Reactive jerker may be bowed (4)

L. The clue Astaire's solved is a classy piece of luggage (7,8)

M. Lepidopterist's dam? (6)

N. Head in back of hut (6)

X. Ancient emperor backs means of reproducing Roman king (6)

O (short). Being rusty, after love and a kiss I perished outside Society (8)

P. Aircraft with involuntary movement wandering in the sky (8)

R. Places available for corruption, wherein a worthy few became thieves (5,2,3)

S. 'Thy servant a dog' (6)

T. Cutter has no alternative at the end (4)

U. Customer for duckling? (4)

PH. I'll approach thin characters with benevolence (15)

CH. Crossworders' consulting rooms? (8)

PS. Crazy one with choice symptoms that are drug-induced (15)

O (long). Sign of momentary significance (4)

Jigsaw No. 4 – GREEK ALPHABETICAL

Jigsaw No. 5 – ALPHABETICAL with a difference

Letters can be used instead of numbers – A=1, B=2, Z=26, etc. The grid is 'lettered'; we have started you off to give you the idea. Solvers also have to fill in the extra thirteen black squares. The clues are numbered for convenience of reference only.

1. African city has one rotten article (6)
2. African's first time – time when I'm not there – to put the bubbles in (6)
3. Bird retires, having eaten headless pachyderm, with diamond (8)
4. Bird with Jack and family's authorised the selfish gene (7)
5. Compounds of amino-acids stimulate movements of the sea (8)
6. Compounds stop with love in making choices (7)
7. Doctor No cross because my Dad and Mum have one different gene (10)
8. Doctor of old, keeping thus to the point, gets petrol (8)
9. Fish after chap with companion in Euphorbia (10)
10. Fish after 10 with Röntgen (1-3)
11. French all-ticket dispenser? (4)
12. French for the year (?) tend to be skinny (4)
13. Lacklustre fashion in which to alter the gait in Evelyn's work (10)
14. Lacklustre partaking of the prize all essentially desire (8)
15. Little creature to be toady (4)
16. Little radiators ooze hail that's melted (8)
17. Motor in which is the last emperor (4)
18. Motor painted (just so) by Kipling (6)
19. Queen that is ugly turned businessman in Ballykissangel (7)
20. Queen's turned sixteen in Paris – have another grab? (2-5)
21. This be the velocity – minus five hundred and fifty in game? I'm not saying (10)
22. Thisbe's 'sweet and lovely' one heard this catcall (4)
23. Unknown one to make allegations about – St Francis (6)
24. Unknown – what did you say? – mutiny by fiddler (6)
25. Watch such stuff when we back a sailor in loathsome surroundings (8)
26. Watch time doubled by Monty's army, the British (5,5)
27. Worried because it's difficult? (6)
28. Worried by endless iniquity in blessed leaders at astronomical angle (144°) (10)

Jigsaw No. 5 – ALPHABETICAL with a difference

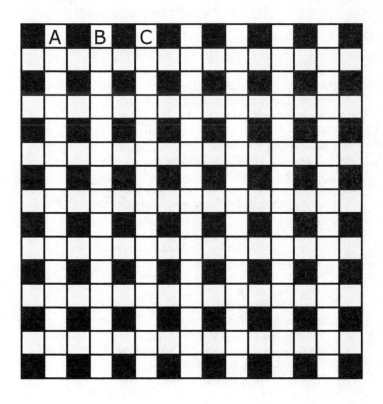

APHORISTICAL JIGSAWS

In the first examples there are words given in the diagram; solutions are to be fitted in with these. In most subsequent examples, the aphorism (or other set of words) is clued; the solution to this is to go in the highlighted squares, and the other solutions fitted in similarly.

Jigsaw No. 6 – APHORISTICAL

1. Get there, and Italians start to say goodbye (6)
2. Hurry up with the skirt hanger (6)
3. It's in Surrey near the ships (7)
4. Back off during feature – it's fine stuff (7)
5. Live to a damned high standard? (5)
6. Euphemia's around, a soldier figures (8)
7. Matchmaker giving us repose (8)
8. It can provide a solution, for once the right one (5)
9. Where the flowers with odd dendrological starters were a' wede away (7)
10. Illuminated lots of lots during escape (8)
11. Referee upset before batting demands non-intervention (4,4)
12. Masculine wiles in the middle (5)
13. Some of Philaret's notes are very funny (9)
14. It's even reversible (5)
15. Sound of senior officer on the warpath? (7)
16. Inseparables in rhyme related to essayist (4,4)
17. Old woodlouse cross about hint to journalist (9)
18. Lubricant and what it does, polluting the seas (3,6)
19. Continuous at time of departure? (7)
20. Indian city with a piece of coconut cake (6)
21. Say No, not a shilling – a pound to top up tank (6)
22. Insectivorous insect, or else leader of bats at belfry (crazy) (6,3)
23. Neptune acts up, hoarding silver (3,3)
24. Muslim greeting in loco? (6)
25. River, one abbreviated amid evaporation? (6)
26. Instil tackling with scraper (7)
27. If he pricks himself in spite of it, let him bleed (7)
28. Sir Herbert (Herb for insider) had three hands (8)
29. Not much to play with (6)
30. Diana, in a Westerly, isn't still like a worm (7)

Jigsaw No. 6 – APHORISTICAL

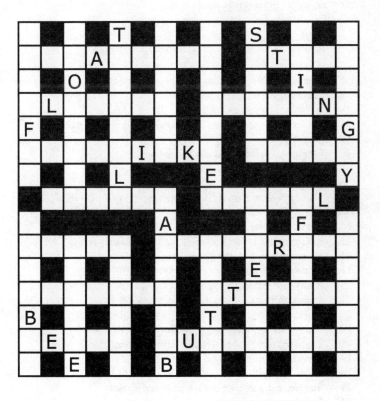

Jigsaw No. 7 – APHORISTICAL

1. A month of bad art (4)
2. Live article in place (4)
3. A song (with backing) (4)
4. A degree exam about love – that's what it is (9)
5. Arrangement for bail due – you'll catch it! (7)
6. See 27
7. Greetings to be on their way to Mayfair ladies (4,6)
8. They resemble millponds – same scale, possibly? Not quite (4,4)
9. Hypocrisy is powerless (4)
10. Vehicle with second letter on for dating (6)
11. Shared space for 10 via lost West African capital between orders of desert (6,4)
12. Dog given its head follows lemon (4)
13. Suggested reading: Medea, not in translation (10)
14. Early days for one joining the EEC (6)
15. Painful feeling from Midlothian stream? (9)
16. It's plain on everyone's back (5)
17. Little girl from 14 16 (4)
18. Stripped for universal viewing, end in trouble (4)
19. To be a home without a book is magic (5)
20. Test for gold and other things (4)
21. Substitute philosophy for sex? Polite answer possible (9)
22. Going on-line could be a trial for composer (4,6)
23. Trust the really heartless (4)
24. Annoy the astronomer, reportedly (4)
25. Damage from the past is almost frightening (4)
26. Investigate refusal in concession (5)
27,6. Grow greater? He proved to be one of the less equal (8)
28. Net broken, you go in to fish with a cast (6-4)
29. End of a tube – Holloway's further (8)
30. Studious students spelt with two Ss (5)
31. Story told in china has little weight (4)
32. Tank-engine's first creator comes cheap (6)
33. Hardy comeback kid, later with musical comeback (3,6)
34. Sound horn fairly hard and hurry for 20 cleaner (10)
35. Cleaner naturally abhorred (6)
36. Lawrence going down will be in Jane's (7)

Jigsaw No. 7 – APHORISTICAL

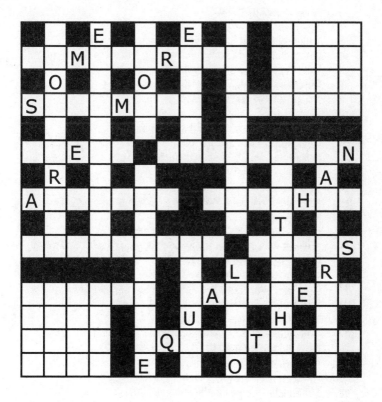

Jigsaw No. 8 – APHORISTICAL

1.   An ancient Roman bulldog reported? (7)
2.   First point is dog or god (6)
3.   Variable part in opera (4)
4.   A case for diplomacy (7)
5.   Sign to show you're watching cricket? (6)
6.   Dog holding sword with point missing will serve drinks (9)
7.   Blind type's brief article on the Thames (9)
8.   Composer's heavy cold? (4)
9.   Yellow type caught by black type (6)
10.   Eat in row no. 5 (4)
11.   Remarkable doers, cats, with or without tails (5-4)
12.   Bill's in, isn't it? – per person (4)
13.   Story about Tory back with distinction (5)
14.   Notes on gala that's decadent (6)
15.   Opera singer topless on island (4)
16.   Footballer (back) for short county with long memory (8)
17.   Woman's right, always (4)
18.   Ape – primate, mostly without sex appeal (7)
19.   Windsor lady, perhaps: firm were worried about her end (5,4)
20.   Food faddist interchanged (8)
21.   In debt, with big deal to fix (9)
22.   Get in the way, which is nothing but non-U and ill-bred (7)
23.   Dance of the honest epicure (3-4)
24.   Man of law sprung from Gingerbread? (9)
25.   State of Denmark? One trend, possibly, in a cat (10)
26.   Party goer without silver – he's devastating (7)
27.   Joint command goes round – Manchester has one (7)
28.   Bonesetters have a name in divisions (7)
29.   The weight of being in Number Ten? (5)
30.   Acquire Jones's partner's tree to make a frame for glass (6-4)

Jigsaw No. 8 – APHORISTICAL

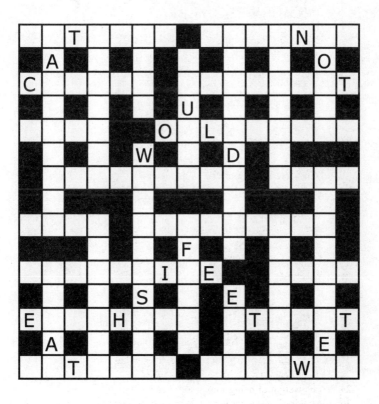

Jigsaw No. 9 – APHORISTICAL

1. Fixed date – about time! – for having absorbed carbon dioxide (7)
2. Dodo known to King David, a scraper without a strike (7)
3. 1 is a first-class left-winger (5)
4. More vigorous, d'you 'ear? Don't cool it! (6)
5. It is 1 with a way with 1 (4)
6. Cables from the top: you're not to get rid of the defender (9)
7. See backroom scientists, in short, about final rocket launches
    (5-4)
8. Students pursue fair-haired actress Joan (8)
9. German city's good French, more or less (4)
10. Voice of ass with vicarious fame (4)
11. Copper joins motoring organisation for a round of drink (7)
12. Princess is partially clad: take your 21 away (9)
13. Fancy mother embracing engineer (5)
14. Extract from 'To hell and back' (Fitzgerald) (4)
15. Support revolutionary seen swallowing beetle (7)
16. Dance or fall out? (6)
17. Come about retreat (Belloc) (7)
18. See one go outside in the snow (5)
19. Characteristic feature of morning in Tenniel's work (9)
20. Island backing strike by volunteers (5)
21. Compiler's keeping one that's needful (5)
22. Free after being changed unawares? (3,5)
23. A way one travels between Afghanistan and India? (6)
24. Artist on board used to have value (7)
25. Polish 14, German spots (7)
26. Some crossword compilers get badgered (4)
27. Pretend Peter's out of ribbon (4)
28. Shut roughly 12 or 13 tricks (4)
29. It's not straight, it's underhand, keeping less than a pound on
    said horse (8)
30. Source of energy on the Southern side (5)
31. To grade is to err, without appropriate backing (8)
32. Increase of power comes second to impulse (5)
33. Diplomatic character gives model performance (4)
34. Some dads get among the playthings at present times (6)
35. African in jug and angry about it (7)
36. Neuter, making mum into nun, possibly (5)

Jigsaw No. 9 – APHORISTICAL

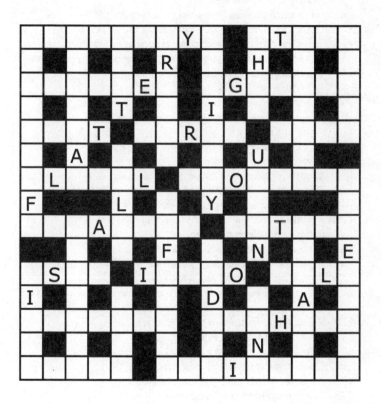

Jigsaw No. 10 – APHORISTICAL

1. Play cabbage, the beach being off, back in the mitred period (6)
2. Badly laid is badly laded (5)
3. Half French greeting, everything and nothing (4)
4. Car driver taking a test, always looking in the mirror? (9)
5. Spanish city in the way of being entered by … (5)
6. … imperfect motorway: be quiet and suffer outside (9)
7. They bar being exposed to a way of learning (2,5)
8. … So many bits of bay, 20 (4)
9. French lady's shrub arrived first in a bad state, getting returned (8)
10. Big bird, a fool in company, gets cautious (9)
11. Wood in Kent (4)
12. Senior in the novel 'Destry rides again' (6)
13. Fine companion? Scots go to the left (4)
14. Style to 16 relief work is one in the lattice (9)
15. Diamonds go into the ring and cubes come out of it (6)
16. I assert my identity having pictures to copy (7)
17. Irregular verb? Not as good at spotting (9)
18. Some food is too coarse for a poet (5)
19. I 16 exactly, putting Latin in a poem in the Sun (7)
20. Answer about Golden Boy, as they say (10)
21. Tory, the side of privilege? That's so (5)
22. Something to do on a pond? Like up to one pound of cereal? (4-5)
23. Rascal fell to fix the contest (10)
24. Showing signs of love in Hebrew (8)
25. Present doctor in riddle with a fallen white mass (9)
26. The Sun is to produce a lone voice (7)
27. Arrest by secret policemen (6)
28. Opening of second front requires cross-timbers (8)
29. The blind prophet wearies one to a point (8)
30. Brown bread for health (5)
31. Beast gets the ill-spoken support (5)
32. Contemporary feeling of enthusiasm about change – I get one (9)

Jigsaw No. 10 – APHORISTICAL

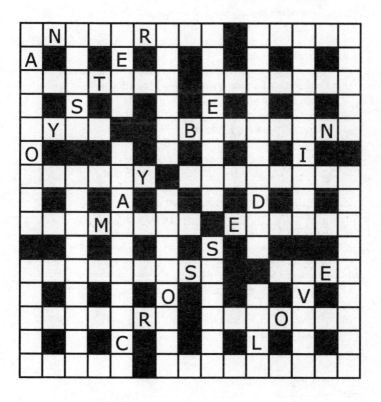

Jigsaw No. 11 – APHORISTICAL

1. Sailor, said to have attacked, was superficially wounded (7)
2. Silver on the 'ead, say? (4)
3. Companion leaving room: don't go! (5)
4. Scene of business (or buzziness), one I pray will change (6)
5. Johnson or Earhart is by way of coming in at farceur Brian (8)
6. Material accident? (5)
7. Doctor Conservative upset is not welcome in the house (3,3)
8. Wader replaces bishop with knight in capital (6)
9. Give Tommy rope – everybody's out of it (5,4)
10. They are pleased to see me in trouble (7)
11. Reverted to 18 when orientals got 16-ed (9)
12. Shade of the 2, the earl, not the poet (4)
13. Don't let anyone see your naked body (4)
14. Hallo! Stop in front of garden or church centre (4,6)
15. It can be jarred, which sounds funny (7)
16. Deceive and take advantage of single member, composer of op. 1 (6,4)
17. (a) (2,3,5,5)
18. They had vassals, for example, part raised between covers (5-5)
19. Boss advancing in progress (7)
20. Return of Marx on TV (5)
21. Academically all a prophet in his own country can get? (4,6)
22. Queen beheaded in place of painter? (9)
23. String players' request to go outside Control Traffic Zone (7)
24. Beast with one horn (5)
25. Leaders of the Right have a voice in Venice (6)
26. Almost all disgrace is bogus (4)
27. He reunited empires: houses do it differently (10)
28. Farceur Ben and Bertie's Aunt Dahlia nearly get cross (7)
29. Natural translation of Plotinus (8)

Jigsaw No. 11 – APHORISTICAL

Jigsaw No. 12 – APHORISTICAL

1. 1 and 1 may be a long time (4)
2. Too partial for impartial solvers? (4)
3. Not where protesters want the dray (8)
4. Child's play for a shepherdess (2-4)
5. What's mortal in Hamlet is anti-natal (4)
6. Signal to amuse the audience by the nail (7)
7. Gather information from returning FBI man about cheese (7)
8. Latter part of school near A2 (4)
9. Letter or letters upset lion (7)
10. The day before she was a bone (3)
11. Right to use of land gives fire over water (3)
12. Insect around home lit up in hard style (8)
13. Secret of reform is not having to pay (4-4)
14. Comedist's caprices, if any nudes are involved (5,5)
15. Saki's stories include half Roald Dahl's (4)
16. New people these days, to use Blair's formulation (10)
17. Skill with figures gives miners time to turn on it (10)
18. Where steamers used to go to make a royal wild (3,7)
19. Proceed without haste to Cranley near Guildford with Hyacinth's brother-in-law (6)
20. Past silica compound in rate that's not general enough (15)
21. Past gunner took in support (9)
22. Choice farm in Barsetshire or South London (9)
23. Tête-à-tête with VIP soldier and theatre goers (7,8)
24. The miller's flower, right one on cape and point (5,3)
25. Receive honour for costume (4)
26. Go away on foot, say (4)
27. Voices make a concession to princess (7)
28. Spotted beak's working to order with tinker about (7)
29. Exchange backhands (4)

Jigsaw No. 12 – APHORISTICAL

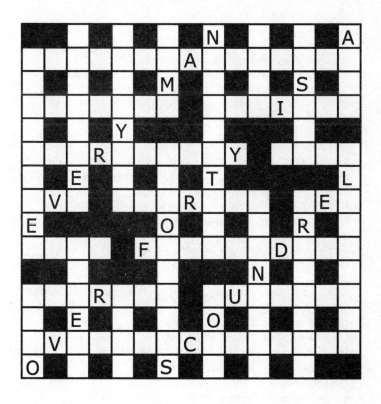

Jigsaw No. 13 – APHORISTICAL

1. Top billing for setter (4)
2. A divine conclusion to a lot of extras (7)
3. Money put on before (4)
4. One lying endlessly on stage (5)
5. A woman tennis player (4)
6. One stupefied (includes one stupefied) (7)
7. Cover for a flier round the pole (6)
8. Nomadic Arabs' port (5)
9. Second Italian painter, more than stupefied (6)
10. Found God among flowers? That's what cowboy did (6)
11. He hasn't volunteered to study the text (9)
12. Letter opener used by raiders (4,3)
13. Compound event, missing quarter deck, by earl (not English) (9)
14. Princess right in parody? This shows otherwise (8)
15. Omit one other feeling (7)
16. Wartime players – some have been saved (4)
17. A small case, exceptionally traumatic, ultimately involving leaders (4)
18. A king's daughter, one that's perished, with one left (7)
19. Clumsy writer is raised in it (5)
20. One supreme in some art? (7)
21. Part of the Ring encompassed by a serpent (musical instrument) (7)
22. Edwin's Scottish heathland (4)
23. Total collapse follows Greek character of mixed race (7)
24. Love, where's the wine? Like a little spot? (7)
25. I have a record: nothing would fall behind (3,3)
26. Where a hat may be advanced (2,5)
27. French soldier turned up imbibing a lubricant (5)
28. Religious leader being quiet about quarrel (7)
29. Torture and abuse on the way up the mountain? (4-4)
30. Small work, drama possibly, of service to traveller (4,3)
31. Cheers in the background? (5)
32. Pension plan gets bad press (5)
33. Wartime precautions with kebab about: fast! (8)
34. Heron with voice of duck sounds like this outside (7)
35. International anglers' ordeal? (4)
36. Destroy a French note (4)

Jigsaw No. 13 – APHORISTICAL

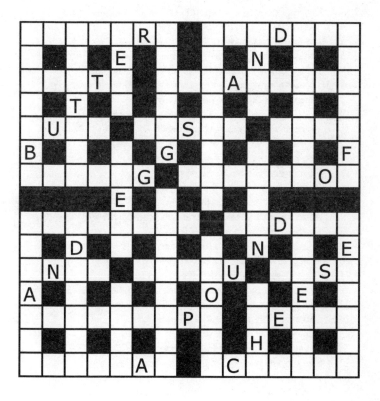

Jigsaw No. 14 – APHORISTICAL

1. Following a measure with hesitation (5)
2. Saint of opera direction (5)
3,23. Live as I do with our support and touching dignity (5,6)
4. Sea was high, hence I got soaked (5)
5. Jag for American girl or boy, say (4)
6. It sounds a happy place (5)
7. Broadsides where negative publicity sticks around (10)
8. S-something wrong in the grounds applied to wounds (9)
9. Taken in at school, we hear (5)
10. Appallingly well-known (say) area, not North America (9)
11. No gene with an exposed figure (8)
12. Return of stake could do a lot of damage (4)
13. Away from the sea, if turning about, for a piece of Sibelius (9)
14. Note to give job back – it's a plum (9)
15. Russian region losing Southern peninsula (6)
16. Maybe subterranean cryptogam in production of anil (8)
17. African king's business dispensing with article (6)
18. Not the gross form of tent (4)
19. Home worth trading in for frontier? (5-4)
20. Medieval halfpence put into bolivars (5)
21. Chap in charge of a little set of 8 (5)
22. Rewritten in old type to make one's meaning clear? (9)
23. See 3
24. Spots the right tree without thinking? (4)
25. Rebellion on the increase? (6)
26. Evangelical footballer to join Hampshire shortly? (5,4)
27. Turning left is strain, sadly, for student (9)
28. Poor man's ski at present in ship next to promontory (4-4)
29. Don't abandon two bits of willow (5,4)
30. Sleuth's false card – got to hold king and queen (7-3)
31. Nearly a catch at pontoon? (6-3)
32. Upholder of partition, strangely (8)

Jigsaw No. 14 – APHORISTICAL

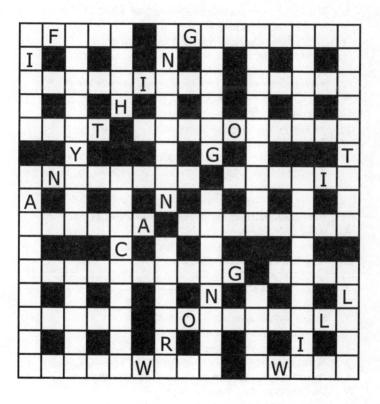

Jigsaw No. 15 – APHORISTICAL

1. A chimney in return for a network? (6)
2. Insect and god make a star (7)
3. Rise from a scene not finished when died (6)
4. Gilded poet loses his top (7)
5. Sir T. Benn – 'e might become a composer (9)
6. A.W., cricketer, produced the willow for yon film (4)
7. Crest broken, telescoped, and burnt in engine (9)
8. Bid me, with crest broken, rebel against the Tsar (10)
9. President's wife is life in Italy (5)
10. It's open to be filled in a piece of land (4)
11. Act (alone) in the matter of thyroid problem (6)
12. Bill singing well? (7)
13. Acquaintances without science don't make great art (6)
14. US city custom – forget it – repulsive outside to an absurd degree (9)
15. Co-operative affair one is a cat about (7)
16. White lady has backed one among the majority of those who belong (3-5)
17. Sweet little creature embracing saint (6)
18. One to look back before finish? (5)
19. Architect of the Louvre flourished briefly before the flood? (8)
20. Something to learn – it's not French weapon that will get you in (8)
21. Black and white clue to 10, possibly? (7)
22. From 30 etc., voting system revolutionised India (7)
23. Sort out eggs for Natasha in War and Peace (7)
24. Miserable is the number giving pain for pleasure (6)
25. Publication in the South is a revolting business (8)
26. Girl graduate from Yemen? (5)
27. Slip in row with dog (7)
28. The month for lobster? (9)
29. Remove sticker from antelope's back with hesitation (5)
30. Positive expression – or negative initially – not long ago (10)

Jigsaw No. 15 – APHORISTICAL

Jigsaw No. 16 – APHORISTICAL

1. Travel firm shows what to do with washing and where (8)
2. See 32
3. Girls' name, one for M. Lamb (6)
4. Horse for the street? (4)
5. Unwilling part of a chapter (6)
6. Shrew's sister goes off in a cab (6)
7. Writer with flower named after him? (4)
8. Oriental going to draw water should have a good meal (3,4)
9. Increase involvement of Che and Anne (7)
10. Flower attractive? Remove head? (7)
11. Rearrange spelling bees – author in the neighbourhood (10)
12. French company among the Irish shortly with even lower temperature (5)
13. Flag seen above (4)
14. Poet of the jigsaw (5)
15. Confess perjury? Even the dead don't always (3,4)
16. Hairs twisted in hands by early rivals to Christians (10)
17. The vehicle wasn't happy (5)
18. Setter's infinitely unintelligent and a learner, as in legend (8)
19. Scandinavian goblin gets money from Japan for hut (6)
20. Infinite qualification? (2,3)
21. Yellow flower late in the day: different one? Different one (9)
22. Most of month replacing Robert in general, being down wind (2,3,3)
23. The first, they say, was Walpole (7)
24. Brought up in Sussex, we hear, on whisky money? (3-5)
25. Strait outside the seaside town (8)
26. Embrace with juicy result? (7)
27. Funny way to the mountains (7)
28. River dangerous: driver needed (3,4)
29. Torture, as the unhandy is to the company (10)
30. Pull top off jersey near Thame, Oxfordshire (8)
31. How to send a monarch depraved around a hill (10)
32,2. At conclusion of speech – usually of action too, as she and I will show (4,3,2,4)

Jigsaw No. 16 – APHORISTICAL

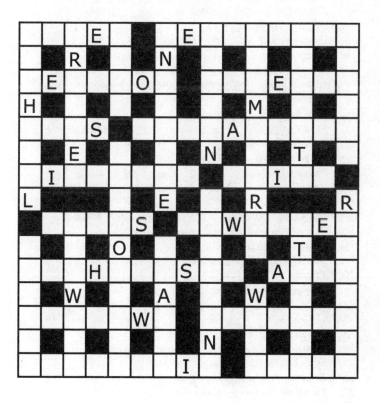

Jigsaw No. 17 – APHORISTICAL

1. Nabal's wife gets a great 'allo (7)
2. Bay of battle with native of Australia, Britain, and Ireland? (7)
3. God's Keats to Shelley (7)
4. Shakespearean wife backing a song by public prosecutor (7)
5. Trojan from Caen, easily distinguished (6)
6. With big businessman losing head is relative (6)
7. Quick, everyone! I'm about right (7)
8. Less than a year in the Julian calendar for housekeeper with ring (7)
9. Attribute to a journalist? (7)
10. One getting married's about – one with sex appeal expected (7)
11. Rat or bow-legged bird is heard (9)
12. Defence for playwright interrupted by bounder (9)
13. Party with animal eating a fen product (9)
14. Shakespearean shepherd makes much of Greek city (5)
15. Be a dilettante like 17? (6)
16. I am gorgeously vague and live in a collector's home (6)
17. Avoids affectionate appellation (5)
18. Speed is a strong point (8)
19. Sir Norman's stag night starts at length (8)
20. The style has some attraction, I concede (5)
21. Christopher's church is in pretty poor taste... (6)
22. ... So's the fire – a record result (3,6)
23. Homo sapiens: it's apparently a religious creature (6)
24. Close supporter held up by marshal (4,2)
25. Stories of the Queen leaving Lover's Lane in turmoil (8)
26. Disposal by ships round Italian port (7)
27. Porcelain is useful upside-down (6)
28. Mountain springs start convulsive movement (5)
29. Loans lubricate the underground (7)
30. Peg holds some wool, showing old-fashioned gratitude (7)
31. Prisoner in unpleasant surroundings in Hamlet? (7)
32. Battles with doctor backed by help from hospital worker (4,4)

Jigsaw No. 17 – APHORISTICAL

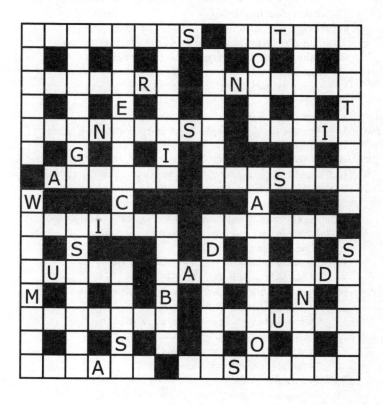

Jigsaw No. 18 – APHORISTICAL

1. Range to measure that need not be fertilised (7)
2. They are against their seniors, as keeping the Teutonic spirit (7)
3. Crafty as well? (4)
4. We hail revolution for a time (6)
5. Little girl's embracing male doctor, the great beasts! (9)
6. There's a giant here, approximately – an eagle (5)
7. Guess how to do tricks without shock treatment (10)
8. King of Persia keeping quiet in a largely Greek situation (6)
9. Oriental that's short at the back (7)
10. Celebrated resurgence from defeats (7)
11. Go among holders of food with holders of drink (7)
12. Old games make the old happy (8)
13. The last of the last of the last of the South Bank? (9)
14. Tyler in revolt, in awkward situation, where punctures are likely? (5,4)
15. Drain rice after cooking with a röntgenising treatment? (10)
16. Chivalrous types of philosopher keeping things dark for queen, right? (7-6)
17. First person to go round the pole was a swimmer (7)
18. Iberian writer, from Portugal or Catalonia (5)
19. Increasingly vocal in the display of ironies (7)
20. What a pity the poem's about hard head and hard heart! (2,4)
21. Address to friend that's precious (4)
22. Small bone's breaking is close (7)
23. Agent of 15 continuing with fabric (5)
24. It's bats to strengthen diamonds (8)
25. Alarmed to find hardcore? (4-5)
26. Opening plant in the home counties without change (6)
27. Addresses in a manner that's archaic and abstracted from M (5)
28. Be quiet for a little: Bond's about, like Elijah (8)
29. Place or hole needed by plants (8)

Jigsaw No. 18 – APHORISTICAL

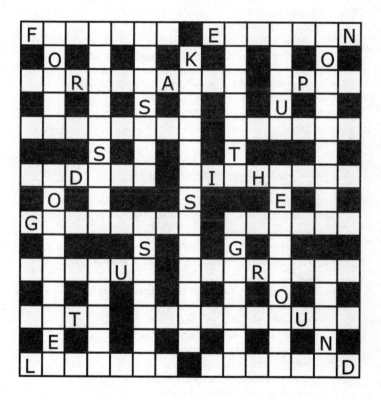

Jigsaw No. 19 – APHORISTICAL

Shaded sqaures: 'In that heaven of their wish …' (5,5,2,2,4,4,3,4).

1. Melody, a girl that frightens the ATC (3-4)
2. Nurse about to rave of fadeless flower… (8)
3. … in which one fled with wool (4)
4. An excessively French home for a beautiful Italian lady (7)
5. Forbid irregular quest for feasts (8)
6. Try to persuade old king about starting a jigsaw (6)
7. Vehicle of Palestinian (say) in accident (almost) (9)
8. Merles – 4 for Christmas – 400 more on top for cuties (5,5)
9. Transpire – and see me sometime? (4,2)
10. Painter in force (9)
11. Calls for tears (5)
12. Continental satellite abducted by bull (6)
13. Guitarist's worry (4)
14. Covers around river for stags (5)
15. Sculptor makes one rhyme or other (5,5)
16. Spanish student abandons West African (7)
17. Italian church in the 7th year? (4)
18. Devotee of writer reported bird when it was dark (7)
19. Preserver of oven returned (6)
20. 'All the world' (when such a maiden marries) sounds like a French writer (5,3)
21. Explaining away from the enemy this month (7)
22. Transport during storm of rain from heaven (7)
23. Frenchies upset so over play (10)
24. Mental problem affecting his company's spy (9)
25. Romance in dream of France with ease (7)
26. Books following change of hero get interrupters (9)
27. Speaker's to get up in the 'ouse taking Iris's part (7)
28. Pod deceases, sadly (4,4)
29. Sir Patrick, republican poet? (5)
30. Prompt means of delivering military requirements (6,4)
31. Continental vegetable (5)
32. Sort how to write? (4)

Jigsaw No. 19 – APHORISTICAL

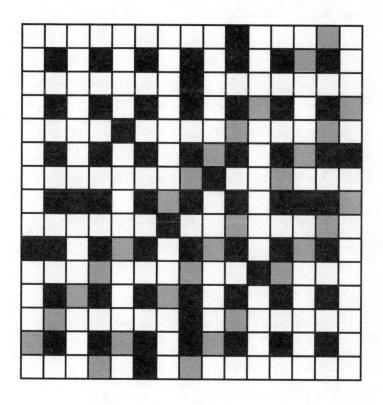

Jigsaw No. 20 – APHORISTICAL

In the shaded squares a Shakespearean lady speaks (in 16) of the varied effects of alcohol (4,5,4,4,4,5,4,4,2,4). The two words that run NW to SE are repeated, and the whole is transcribed in the most natural way possible.

1. Old-fashioned, with thought for mental reservation (7)
2. Cocked 'at yonder, on day off (2,3,5)
3. Physical exercise? Car's outside! (8)
4. Is it right to be implanted in animal? (6)
5. Make tea, as told, to laughter and excitement (8)
6. Presents rebel to the French (7)
7. Reduction at local shop's opening won't do a thorough job (3,7)
8. Split work of handyman drinking lighter vermouth? (8)
9. Opening, then die? (4)
10. Give money to French boy that doesn't open the church (6)
11. Vassal turns up at musical, which is invigorating (5,3)
12. Flue constructed for fire (4)
13. Attempt with strip of wood to enclose one giant (7)
14. Rodent would quickly duck (6)
15. Jew born among her partners (6)
16. I live and have shortly interrupted diffuse scribe along the usual lines (6,5)
17. Like Olde England – am I wrong in myself? (6)
18. Alternative nasals are standard (4)
19. Funny fellow to love lovely body, about five hundred strong (3,4)
20. Poems as returned to port (6)
21. Here are homes with a capital H (6)
22. Great destruction (8)
23. Support for visit (4)
24. What creative achievements come up leading to Panama? (5,3)
25. It's prevalent after street fighting (6)
26. Disreputable and somewhat viscous (5)
27. Prudent with a new head? At a stretch it could be (8)
28. Small farmers get solvers with sheikdom on line (8)

Jigsaw No. 20 – APHORISTICAL

Jigsaw No. 21 – APHORISTICAL

Shaded squares: O Euro-victory in top of arm on bed (single): Scottish river, English trees, teetotal setters: precedents are always undesirable (7,6,4,2,4,3, 3,5,4).

1. A place where graduates eat can be reduced (8)
2. Time for the silver tablet? (3)
3. Proverbial elevator – gin at the chemist's? (9)
4. Dear good soul, one learning to be in company (6)
5. Cry, young Miss Spooner – hope you can swim! (4,5)
6. Fish general up (3)
7. Weapon of the peerage (4)
8. I hamper development of OT character (7)
9. Fat lazy ample bloke's leading characteristic (4)
10. Pink musicians using old Y-fronts to start with (5)
11. Peach, for example, French – see returning quality (9)
12. Travel at 100 mph was successful (3,2)
13. Californian city and any other for eponymous Trollope heroine (4,4)
14. See through person with long strides (5)
15. Setter under chimney shows surprise (5)
16. Demi-astronomer with almanac (5)
17. Separate backing for Iron Age general (7)
18. Paper for hardly sober parson to back (8)
19. Low-scoring match? That makes ten (3-6)
20. Evident round object reaching the green (5)
21. Paradoxical instrument (10)
22. Locality containing one fish (6)
23. Gas for glass? (7)
24. The sort to be a Sapper? Make a fair copy (6)
25. Second prize in cricket for Windows? (6)
26. Deal with river turning round (3,2)
27. Things that can be commenced with astrological data … (4, 6)
28. …. which appear in tax point, as Tusitala did (4,1,4)
29. Spots Conservative in light brown collecting garbage (5-3)
30. Disapproving remark by alternative teacher (5)
31. Second price on Good Friday? No way 10p will be enough (3,1,5)

Jigsaw No. 21 – APHORISTICAL

Jigsaw No. 22 – APHORISTICAL

COMPO, CLEGG and FOGGY are to be placed symmetrically in the diagram.

1. Cathedral city famed for its odour and need for a wash (7)
2. Obscurity in Chambers gives opportunities for development (9)
3. Archaeologist's work dealing with ship to go off the point (7)
4. Millennium experience? — a favour! (4)
5. But they aren't worn on the chest (7)
6. Base elements, say, in the medical profession (5)
7. Humble pie would do as well for the casually attired (3,4)
8. Directions about horse said to have been laid (4)
9. King with no family and king that couldn't cook, from the Wizard (7)
10. With large-scale measures, some large odes I composed (8)
11. Revised rating about the Entertainer, a spooky old film (5,5)
12. Marry here and one would back the social worker to have some work (6)
13. Dirty rubbish with ferns in the lovesome garden (4)
14. Money for trade unionists? (8)
15. It goes to pot – i.e. the gallows? (4)
16. Peter at bridge with an old shoe (4-3)
17. Setter 'as three wickets in three balls, we 'ear, making him feel better? (6)
18. To commend to favour, we hear she dressed in grey for dinner (10)
19. Queen over Los Angeles? I'll help if you're awash with money (9)
20. District in the home ... of Arabs etc. (4,4)
21. Fabric for painting a QC? (3-4)
22. My share is suet pudding: part is put out again (7)
23. Obstinacy of spirit – around it is hogwash (4-4)
24. Native American playwright's maiden name (7)
25. Shakespearean murder victim strips on return (5)
26. Objections raised to counterfoil (4)
27. Change beater (6)
28. Means of operating steam yacht at the front (6)
29. High notes by clown impersonating priest (5)
30. Remain in one of the Western Isles? (4)
31. Pathetic little bits of pastry? (7)

Jigsaw No. 22 – APHORISTICAL

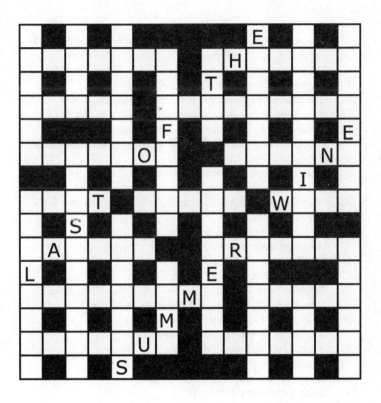

Jigsaw No. 23 – APHORISTICAL

There are two sweets in the shaded squares, clued thus: Slip is one that's left off the front page, one held by librarian (11,3,3). Repeatedly teach old boy wrong (5,2,9).

1. Sailors and spare-time soldiers get home – or don't (7)
2. Appalling infant of limited size topped and tailed (7)
3. What's more, they are dead and done for (7)
4. Battle to gain one inch without halt (7)
5. Cheer return of a record in a second course (7)
6. Inform about article to view critically (8)
7. Graduate and how he may be distinguished in early years (8)
8. Led Zeppelin starts first to leave, deceived by woody grass (6)
9. Cradles for fish (first catches) (9)
10. Loud, vulgar, asinine sound surrounds the ship (6)
11. Mass of blue skins shifted (9)
12. Watchman loses his head on access (5)
13. No sole cause to relax (6)
14. 21 3 includes cause to flip (6)
15. Shakespearean mischief makes precinct resound (8)
16. Servant from Ulster during repast (6)
17. Zero volume last month for the paranormal (6)
18. Start taking rough notes (5)
19. About a hundred loathe Shakespeare's call to hounds (7)
20. Ground that's raised after cart or part (5)
21. Gin and port went quickly in confidence trick (8)
22. Painter with sound of frying bacon? (6)
23. Volatile Sal crept like a ghost (8)
24. Wager for burning? (5)
25. Soaks precipitous places (6)
26. Taoiseachs' deputies with unaccountable things outside in a mess (9)
27. Believer takes lead in train robbery (6)
28. Fool at church makes convulsive movement (6)
29. Said not to be in the manner of the cinematic brothers making a release (9)
30. Anonymous letters from North Dakota genius (8)

Jigsaw No. 23 – APHORISTICAL

Jigsaw No. 24 – APHORISTICAL

The shaded squares on the top and bottom lines contain 28s (4; 4; and 8); the others have mere followers (6; 6; and 5).

1. A bit of organisation that's skilful (5)
2. Long periods containing Nathaniel's relations (7)
3. Solitary confinement? There's nothing in it: it's a piece for a single stringed instrument (5,4)
4. Chanel a crazy person? Just shy (7)
5. Thus (all women do) with lettuce first (4)
6. Bird catcher on top of peer? (7)
7. Go in and use material formed by fire (7)
8. Scottish suspect's last to second the intolerant of rivalry (7)
9. Young animal, a heavyweight, where the Geordie worm operated (7)
10. Prepares for burial: makes investment (4,3)
11. Yearn for acknowledgment of old weapon (7)
12. Scottish rowing boats with advertisements for body fluid? (8)
13. Home straight with no house (4)
14. Be senior to organiser of a turn in authority (7)
15. Mannerist painter at French bridge, a golden moment (8)
16. Being monarch without turning up is off-putting (9)
17. Words of consent to arrangement, hour to hour (5-2)
18. More than a little doubtful about monarch's property (7)
19. 20 polish with broom, perhaps (5)
20. Playing chess and sleep make you silent (10)
21. Observe the mark (4)
22. Scales used by South as West (7)
23. Jack's line on a heap of stalks (5,5)
24. Thoroughfare, one with an actor in it (6)
25. Harrow school trampers make the score with time for ladies (3,6-3,3)
26. Newcomer keeps article in Italian town near the Swiss border (6)
27. Extremely hawkish way of cajoling tourist with one for nothing (5-10)
28. Quality in which Keats's name was … (5)
29. … a summons (4)

Jigsaw No. 24 – APHORISTICAL

Jigsaw No. 25 – APHORISTICAL

The shaded squares form a Marxist law: always refuse a shoot on a regular holiday (5,4,1,6,2,4,5).

1. Periods treated as one (5)
2. Dispatch, say, returned in like seniority (8)
3. Frenchman's drink put into beer belly's (6)
4. Flower on pole at the back (6)
5. Intriguing party taking part of Spanish gentleman (5)
6. None in North Italian city following this French NCO (9)
7. Weapon with members (4)
8. Meet in the middle and don't let your mind wander at departing (9)
9. Stoop to Hamlet's speech? (5)
10. Coke, perhaps, in parliament with doctor and writer? (4-5)
11. Elizabeth I in besides (5)
12. Detective I reported? (3)
13. Put a little melted ghi first in the cooker – then you'll need a second (5,1,4)
14. Reddish-brown rodent in the back if continuing being thwarted (10)
15. Balmy person? I'm first in the self-catering cottage (9)
16. King in the West, tea-maker in Russia, mostly English, is playing chess (5,1,4)
17. Audacity on the railway is higher in the winter (8)
18. Back row to acquire old fool (6)
19. Number 13 – yen for destruction? (6-5)
20. Small coin for butter maker? (6)
21. Weather heard to prevail? (4)
22. Venerers may be upset, being old-fashioned (8)
23. Nonsense language, with the last letter after the first, is like a pig after truffles (8)
24. Almost ill? Quite so (3)
25. Drink – not fast, they say – there's a trap (4,3)
26. All right then, cry 'tie-break' (6)
27. Gaiters dressed with bristles (7)
28. It's impressive out (8)
29. A slight taste of metal on the new cruet (8)
30. One in a region with three rays (6)

Jigsaw No. 25 – APHORISTICAL

DIAMETRICAL JIGSAWS

Solutions for the diameters are to be placed in the highlighted squares. The other solutions are to be fitted in with them.

Jigsaw No. 26 – DIAMETRICAL

Diagonally from the top left-hand corner: Third person not wanted with a weight of garnet (10-5). From the bottom left-hand corner: Critical sound wave makes ice cream (9,6).

1. Sailor services digests (7)
2. Feed or read about name for a Poole Harbour island (8)
3. Run at speed along the path of life? (6)
4. Expression of amazement about 'ateful indoor path (8)
5. Sorry steed's perished craft (10)
6. Divine direction in quantity of medicine (5)
7. Facilitates taking part in routine as established (5)
8. Fall asleep, possibly (6)
9. 45 inches for a girl's name (4)
10. Three quarters in various quantities compose an old Jewish ascetic (6)
11. Lot about referee having trouble with low cholesterol (3-4)
12. Mechanic in comparatively good health (6)
13. The composer seems happy to be at Munchen (8)
14. Declaration asserting the primacy of feelings? (6,3,6)
15. Peer quick to make invocation (4,5)
16. Mother's incursion into trunk, possibly (4,4)
17. Greeting inverted by cry of dismay (1,4)
18. Alternatively, have a meal with ecstasy – I'm taking orders (7)
19. Fight against traveller with new gun (6)
20. A little swift, not being crazy about Alan Greenspan's lead (9)
21. Branded state visible after Macbeth's hand was dipped? (10)
22. Female with a genealogy that produces butter (4-4)
23. Walk pompously in support (5)
24. Desire in location for rock (7)
25. Touching miscegenator looks right in a fez (3-5)
26. Machiavellian work by Pinter, Che being involved (3,6)
27. Having long locks, three entered by ship (6)
28. See 6 before we turn up (4)
29. Muppet, raw with maltreatment, makes device for engine (5,4)

Jigsaw No. 26 – DIAMETRICAL

Jigsaw No. 27 – DIAMETRICAL

Diagonally from the top left-hand corner: Blend of two plays by the same author – one taught by a teacher (7,8). From the top right-hand corner: Play about dress – about Botticelli in a coat (5,10).

1. Italian poet beheaded in Italian town (6)
2. Compress its cart, possibly (7)
3. French town to fall without M (5)
4. Prejudiced people reached during encore (6)
5. Aviator after some trouble finds disturbance (7)
6. Gulf made by prince with M   (5)
7. Ancient city, wrongly dated, circumnavigated by eel that has taken deliberate risks (7,6)
8. I'd erred badly, being a sorrowful girl (7)
9. Philanthropist's friend round river (2-6)
10. Returning actor Gérard's part is covered (6)
11. Swallow claptrap? (3,5)
12. Corn found in wood (5)
13. Top professorship for babysitter? (4,5)
14. Versifier says he is … is going into telecommunications firm (7)
15. It is used in a trick – for a period in an illusion (6,4)
16. The man next the magpie (5)
17. Prepare to start journey of ten inches? (6)
18. Thriller writer Gavin in family alliance (5)
19. Geological discontinuity at the doctor's house (4)
20. Lord Peter Wimsey's assistant falls (9)
21. Negative part of part of London: we shan't pay their debts! (8)
22. Old alphabet put next the crypt by Linnaeus (4)
23. Finished book of Bible – Ham's? (8)
24. Hop off before Lady Asquith returns to take a picture (9)
25. Southern sea, nothing but red wine? (5)
26. Dry region, first part of 15, is difficult, and setter's upset about it (4,6)
27. Can broken leg have pins and needles? (6)
28. French singer is English when in English river (6)
29. Educational post requires trip South (9)

Jigsaw No. 27 – DIAMETRICAL

RHOMBICAL JIGSAWS

Solutions for the rhombus are to be placed in the highlighted squares, beginning at the centre of the left-hand side of the diagram. The other solutions are to be fitted in with them.

Jigsaw No. 28 – RHOMBICAL

Rhombus: Identities in Pope's (often misquoted) warning to students (1,6,8: 1,9,5).

1. Flamboyant craft with a hole in it (7)
2. Fish go round island at the bottom (5)
3. Tessa for baroness of the jet set? – credit for the broke? (10)
4. It's not unprecedented with Libra's effect (7,3)
5. US VP Aaron's accent was hard to get rid of (4)
6. Player on game show sat out and was happy about it (10)
7. Thick skin of Queen gets all the business? (7)
8. Exposes pretensions of French beds (7)
9. Blonde with trim figure leads to high tension, all above the belt (4,5)
10. Cryptogam in hell? (4)
11. Fat fairy returned and abandoned (7)
12. Song about caliph at sea in church (7)
13. Bond's girl lapped up everything initially (4)
14. Version of Lycidas as replaced by one student of poetry (7)
15. Original resemblance is self-reflected by the Big Apple (7)
16. Enlightened him about uranium being the lightest metal (7)
17. Spielberg's discovered what Doyle originally mislaid (4,5)
18. Lake of fodder (7)
19. The song of the seriously rich? (5)
20. Bouquet the hearer is familiar with? (4)
21. Left to mount in Surrey (7)
22. Kin to treadle operator (7)
23. Outstanding works of the Royal Institute are placed sixth (7)
24. Big tree makes endless ring in water (7)
25. Lebanese town that's fathered by Eugene Goossens (7)
26. Unstudied soup – something wrong with recipe – get wine waiter (9)
27. New town gets on terms in the theatre (9)
28. Royal crumpet in cake? (7)

Jigsaw No. 28 – RHOMBICAL

29. It sounds like the enemy of the herb garden (5)
30. Ahab's game, mixing with sheep without prince (5,5)
31. It's more perverse to go to the extremities of water without whiskey (5)
32. Yorkshire and England cricketer wanting length and line (7)

Jigsaw No. 29 – RHOMBICAL

Rhombus: Two persons near the top of their respective professions together produce maternity challenge, or a fair share (3-5-7; 8-7).

1. First love gets on line, being under pressure (7)
2. A solvent from heaven (6)
3. This affliction can make everything horribly grey (7)
4. Gore's commonplace benevolence (8)
5. Something for the foot, not the head, like this introduction to something more (3,4)
6. Members leading people into undesirable competition (4,4)
7. Having aesthetic tastes, he forsakes the opposite type (4)
8. A straggler's fodder plant, so to speak? (10)
9. I work in the kitchen after the game (6)
10. I had precedence, say, in latrines – things that go with soldiers? … (6,4)
11. … It takes two months, but I should stop after three and a half minutes! (6)
12. Flat found late in the day? (4)
13. Franco's awful lot, admitting – nay, generating – evil leaders (7)
14. The Dame of Rio? (6)
15. See 22
16. Demon lord to decorate costermonger? (7)
17. This American glamour may be subject to tabulation (10)
18. Revolutionary has not paid monarch – this one will run and run (10)
19. Lady of the Raj eats pork the wrong way, causing a lot of resistance (6)
20. Regrettably plump girl entertaining one who needs time to be entertained (8)
21. Love the sunrise? One has to bear it (4)
22,15. Opening for sailors whose harbour's an unpleasant place (8)
23. Piece of fleece? (4)
24. Vexatious subjects exhibiting too in press (4,6)
25. Spur fits round chimney when it's put up (8)
26. Bun-fight with players taking food, we hear (3,7)
27. Set out to enter genuine person to be relied on (7)
28. Some of Lucy's ways involved rotund characters (6)

Jigsaw No. 29 – RHOMBICAL

Jigsaw No. 30 – RHOMBICAL

Rhombus: 'World without end' (11,4) with 'God the Trinity?' (7,8).

1. Motor among first-class arachnids (5)
2. One with profit: one with profit (5)
3. Back number is in time to suffer (7)
4. Vent linking a rat with fish? (8)
5. In general man accounts for annual publication (7)
6. Heath stars with capital prosecutor (9)
7. Graduate thus acquires computer language (5)
8. Devotee taking purgative drug to cattle (9)
9. Turtle, the Lone Ranger, eaten by Greek islander (with some wine) (9)
10. Lived to the end of the world – the German world (5)
11. John on the line to the North (5)
12. Lancashire hill topped by Hitler's men, like the rhombus? (7)
13. Dye among Galileo's ingredients (5)
14. Milk carrier goes round about bringing good wishes (7)
15. Cook eating rodent in dining-room (6)
16. Priestley reported from the top of the two top stories (reportedly) (8)
17. Monkey in the style of antelope (6)
18. Sloth has its moments (7)
19. Beg removal from starter, the man in the middle? (5)
20. Fame of the wrong sort brought ire to Tony (9)
21. Paul, say, without a P, has right as groom (6)
22. Not Ernie who partnered Eric? (9)
23. Love and truth curtailed? Hopefully you'll get — (4,2)
24. Defence against demons confined to Broadland village (8)
25. Let in again to study with German (7)
26. High pressure in cold storage (not Fahrenheit) (5)
27. Sown in a chair about half a minute (9)
28. Long, long to look round the lake (7)
29. New baby once found in teacup (8)
30. There's tea brewing for Doll (9)
31. Model 1099 in link with birds (7)
32. Latin in a year in Palestinian port? Cruel! (9)

Jigsaw No. 30 – RHOMBICAL

Jigsaw No. 31 – RHOMBICAL

Rhombus: Carol's seasonal greeting, second part abbreviated (3,4,3,5, 5,2'1,4,3).

1. Behaves badly, exchanging tops of tomato sauce (4,2)
2. A silent vowel, keeping quiet – one who's lost a part (7)
3. Abolish American ring (7)
4. Mushy peas round the back? (4)
5. How a good guy should go on a horse? (7)
6. Stew with white sauce keeping the French warm in bed? (10)
7. Isn't a split second enough to make a singer? (10)
8. The thing is that after depression you get tummy trouble (7)
9. Italian political leader backed this number, a catholic (5)
10. Give a dog a bad name – gone off with a churl (10)
11. The last spike for absence to do? (6)
12. Nuts when surrounded by previous class boss (4,6)
13. Extraordinarily regal look (5)
14. Cricketer's prize – the last toast? (5,3)
15. Pollster's in building to wag (8)
16. One with two ears, could it mean? This is stupid (7)
17. First French person to have a rotten feeling of distrust (8)
18. Anagram for sale? (6)
19. Retreat left to the breeze (4)
20. Samite's woven by painter (7)
21. So loth to leave David's son and vanquished foe in the East (8)
22. In polo he could be the one with the palate (8)
23. Frank's scheme for getting rid of partition? (4-4)
24. Flower circle gets custom (4)
25. Paternal attempt at baking? (6)
26. Whine about ten-year opening of Bath bridge (8)
27. Composer sounding satisfied with little room (7)
28. A lot of sheets – about fifty – in the field (5)
29. Write your name or a cross? (4)
30. It prevents publication of report (8)
31. Gamble on different way of painting irises (7)
32. Take pole to duck (5)

Jigsaw No. 31 – RHOMBICAL

Jigsaw No. 32 – RHOMBICAL

Rhombus: The beginning of the proverb about gold (3,4,8) and its consoling corollary, vulgarly expressed by a 'novice in a pinny that's adapted ceremonies' (4,4,7).

1. Intruders take tritium and iodine from slaughterhouses (7)
2. Proverb about quiet writer's attachment (9)
3. Polonius's cover for embarrassment (5)
4. Poison at work in round robin's opening (7)
5. Lost on board? (2,3)
6. Dance about for a second in exchange (7)
7. Breakdown of pet, a secretive creature, outside society (9)
8. Caller from Rio in extended family? (7)
9. Singer moving to Carlton (9)
10. US state not at home to huntress (5)
11. Bathe with model and time flies (7)
12. In former times, a tart that's open to the spirit world (7)
13. Any reported publicity for Muses and morris men, for example? (7)
14. Look at the neckwear of vulgar Romans (7)
15. Abnormal opening of closed hand with 'oop (7)
16. Plantation owner in service first (5)
17. Cleaner holding types of feeble fellow (7)
18. Almost teetotal setter, Araucaria, when curiously the dog did nothing (5-4)
19. It's played on a pail without a player (7)
20. Page in black and white paper is a fantasy (4,5)
21. A wanderer concerned with energy, its bark is thin (5,4)
22. After what sounds fresh as hay I have a breathing problem (9)
23. Bright red mineral in genuine paperback? (7)
24. Little Woman in atmosphere raised by wine (5)
25. Great novelist! (5)
26. Abashed, being old-fashioned, by false disposition of fates (9)
27. Training place for comedian with boy around (7)
28. Draw to the side to secure rafters (3,4)
29. Uncle Joe's drunk (3,4)
30. Composited by petty lunatic outside the home counties (7)
31. Use unprofitably what sounds central (5)
32. Sidney and Beatrice worked wonders with salad (5)

Jigsaw No. 32 – RHOMBICAL

PERIMETRICAL JIGSAWS

Around the perimeter of the diagram, read clockwise from the top left-hand corner, unless otherwise stated, goes a quotation, aphorism, or phrase(s) to which a clue is given; the other solutions are to be fitted in with them.

Occasionally the perimeter works differently: where this is so, the puzzle is labelled 'Perimetrical (Variant)' and further instructions are given.

Jigsaw No. 33 – PERIMETRICAL

Perimeter: Acceptability – ask gross Yank FDR to produce his cousin's advice (5,6,3,5,1,3,5).

1. A quarter having dresses need oxygen (7)
2. The infinite God 10 disoriented? Completely so (3,2,3)
3. A quiet part of an Italian region being cool (6)
4. Skill of 22's namesake (10)
5. Fish: change them to household pest (6-4)
6. Shed enters new clew: put one out for a guest (5,5)
7. Opposed to a journey without ups and downs? (7)
8. The facts about the old city are poison (6)
9. Girl to act to protect the kingdom (4)
10. Somewhere as remote as the orient (4)
11. Clothes to be changed? (4)
12. Too much of a sticky start? (4)
13. Progression of note showing damage by icon-oclasm? (8)
14. Policeman Sir Peter, a deserted village model (6)
15. Draw deeply on fag? Not quite – as one may be cut (2,4)
16. Very dark, like Brighton Rock youth at Armentières (4)
17. King goes to extremes in a loudspeaker, which is suicidal (8)
18. Cat's-paw for some kind of people (4,3,3)
19. Suits cat eating cat without hesitation at first (10)
20. Unjustly gaoled for seniority? (3,3)
21. Hint at following page with spots (6)
22. Hood's faithless girl adds colour to the Army (5,5)
23. Transport has an effect outside, where it's grassy (8)
24. Western snake in the round featuring Old Man River (8)
25. A 24 part 2 within another, to be vague (7)
26. A range of treatments that heal psychic wounds (3,4)
27. Not scared to attack after a fun caper (8)
28. Question from point to cover? (4)

Jigsaw No. 33 – PERIMETRICAL

Jigsaw No. 34 – PERIMETRICAL

Perimeter: Propositions about profit we reconstructed with division holding back law in Gateshead (sang Frank's girl Nancy) (5,5,4,4,3,7).

1. Sound sleeper's wakener from railroad in the morning (5-5)
2. Priest and servers make a record about a sailor of aesthetic character (5,5)
3. Declare Greek character is initially manifesting belief in a world-soul (10)
4. Lake – like a sound to be played (4)
5. Born upper-class in equality – check this rich Tory material (4,6)
6. Shout down, with right, a coarse fellow (4)
7. He can testify to hearing waiter upset head (3-7)
8. Get rid of most of the Times (4)
9. Sweetheart's heart is easy for Spenser (4)
10. Reds failed dismally to form united states (10)
11. Induced poet to rebel and act as first piglet (2,2,6)
12. Housework has to be got through (4)
13. Holdups in the jaw are the devil with loudspeakers (10)
14. Does dough need to be? (7)
15. Romantic line sent back (4)
16. Student in love to be put down (4)
17. Bloodhound left food in ground (4)
18. Opening of multicoloured ice far from spring (4)
19. American responsibility? (4)
20. The breath of advertising? (4)
21. Seat outside old city, sixth in range (7)
22. Old poet of infinite heaven, name of John (7)
23. Old-fashioned policemen are two-dimensional (6,4)
24. Pressure to construct emporium (10)
25. Chips are all right in 10, a day before you get up (5-5)
26. A purged revolutionary put on higher level (7)
27. Dry bed, this time in Mayfair (4)
28. One or more of a herd now heard in Scotland? (10)

Jigsaw No. 34 – PERIMETRICAL

Jigsaw No. 35 – PERIMETRICAL

The perimeter transported people from 1923 to 1948 (6,3,5-7,7).

1. A girl I love on the Riviera (7)
2. A story for people experiencing estrangement (10)
3. Consumption by the Irish among joiners and insectivores (3-5)
4. An abstemious general became prime minister (6)
5. Transport gold to an American bay (10)
6. Go back by pole in boat, to see friends on parade (3-4)
7. The lake sounds weird (4)
8. Unusual topic in converse: take it up and have a look (10,5)
9. Grass is fine stuff (4)
10. What's black and silver in the French connection (7)
11. Obituary for corgi clone, possibly (10)
12. North Germany's first lamp (6)
13. It's pleasant on the Riviera (4)
14. Holiday delivery? (3-5)
15. Maverick politician's not in charge of artist's medium (3-5)
16. In full flight: none hurt, surprisingly (2,3,3)
17. Part of the Bible is given to regrets (4)
18. Quiet, everybody, or you'll get that ghost look (6)
19. Take from 17 and insert 100 in the study of Daleks? (8)
20. Country of H. H. Munro, holding back small book and article (8)
21. Saint's desire for minimum clothing (6)
22. Do African antelopes return to Ra? (3-3)
23. Far from gifted story about fast ship (10)
24. Flier 'as lift-off from supporter of Marshal (7)
25. Where one's pipped at the post, for the opposite direction to the perimeter (8,7)
26. Two little people back with bill for woodwork (6)

Jigsaw No. 35 – PERIMETRICAL

Jigsaw No. 36 – PERIMETRICAL

Perimeter: What Scrooge wanted to be, and in a sense succeeded (4,6,3,6,2,7).

1. TUVWXYZ is sweet (6)
2. Treacle's duff in Warwickshire (8)
3. FBI man left in charge between articles associated with Canterbury (8)
4. Revolutionary garment from 20 for a skunk (4)
5. Sound of singer killed to encourage the others (4)
6. Cavaliere servente: Roman orator briefly lives to live on love (8)
7. Number of Dalmatians having links with Dickensian two (6)
8. Not pleased with genealogies that are placed on masts (10)
9. Number issue wrongly: neglect will ensue (6)
10. English painter among Scots off course with big stinger (5-3)
11. 0–51 in code is very primitive (8)
12. Stop and think (4)
13. Henry competes on track with rodents (7)
14. Badly cooked pie with nuts and oil (6)
15. Siege expecting returns (10)
16. Home is within the preserve of Indian religion (7)
17. Scene of force feeding is chaos (4)
18. Leg legally placed (6)
19. Goddess poetically coming into people brings illumination (8)
20. Cadet or potential soldier (7)
21. Rest-cure, sloppily reported, is a saviour (7)
22. Transport tutor from RADA? (10)
23. Made stable for horse about 2002 years ago (8)
24. Start, of course, with toffee? (3,3)
25. Majority – 60 per cent of seats – with scrolls (3,4,3)
26. Poet identifies parson going the other way (5-3)
27. Solvers that sound to be seeking attention (3-3)
28. Solvers from Southern USA and everywhere else? (3-3)

Jigsaw No. 36 – PERIMETRICAL

Jigsaw No. 37 – PERIMETRICAL

Perimeter: Mary Bennet's dismissal from the pianoforte (3,4,9,2,4,6).

1.   Pudding possesses fragrance for men (10)
2.   Indigo's encompassing mother and creatures (7)
3.   Support, with reason, the environment (10)
4.   French furniture is a game to the audience (4)
5.   Not the civil list, or else one-off Winston's about (6,4)
6.   Getting together? A trick, nearly? (10)
7.   Always keeping a horse, reportedly, student used to deal in layings (6)
8.   The brain can help one work (10)
9.   Access as a matter of course (6)
10. There's no remains of the day, mate (6)
11. Sticky stuff, reverse of logarithm for large number (6)
12. Mother, abandoning magic, managed it inside like Aberdeen (8)
13. A companion article in the border of Norfolk (7)
14. The man has to cook slowly – to make it kosher? (8)
15. Bolshevik in silent revolution (8)
16. Behold attempt at identification (4)
17. Harry on the Wye rather than at Sedgemoor? (8)
18. It's in the South of France, to be exact (4)
19. Half of triple triplet isn't 26 (3-1)
20. Norman bishop takes ours off, getting up our noses? (7)
21. It has 'golden lamps in a green night' – maybe eat green or (preferably, the gold) (6,4)
22. Polar head putting on to polar bear (10)
23. Italian poet, not French, with a genus of bacterium (7)
24. Elicit most of Bobby Shafto's destination following coma (4)
25. Island(s) taken by the conquistadores (4)
26. Top form? (5,5)
27. South-East Asian tagged with 'armis'? (4)
28. Time for agreement, right? (4)

Jigsaw No. 37 – PERIMETRICAL

Jigsaw No. 38 – PERIMETRICAL

Perimeter: Proverbially prince on river with fool excels aristocrat at study (4,1,4,2,6,4,2,5).

1. Atypical slip by the mouth of – food? (10)
2. A fairy with another ten helps one to go (8)
3. Skill without information isn't as good as gold (6)
4. Divine form of maestri (7)
5. Gracious pilgrim was an endless comedian (4)
6. Waiting for dancing? (10)
7. Term used on Norfolk waters for a weapon (10)
8. Sacks Hazel for losing his scut? (5,5)
9. A little rush taken from rear hide (hind skin?) (4-4)
10. A set for a rise? (4)
11. Distant tool for lawn contains tonic for dishonest traveller (4,6)
12. The boy is after a coin (7)
13. Preliminary contest in the kitchen … (4)
14. … insufficiently apparent in ice and cocktail in the region of Vientiane (10)
15. Scotland yard man detects a fiddle in US general (8)
16. One thousand pound on exterior organ (4)
17. Plenty to restrict a little girl (6)
18. Being a detective, discover what embraces birds in 'La Belle Dame sans Merci' (6)
19. Drug covers supporter for nationalised transport with shame (10)
20. Archduke or engineer, either way (4)
21. Betelgeuse is a left-wing emblem (3,4)
22. Phrase translated into Nepalese (6)
23. Expression of regret from Kumasi, Ghana (4)
24. Croatian slave-owners' region? (8)
25. Physical condition of reliable citizen? Note – it lasted out (5-5)
26. Colour one found in explosive (4)
27. Remove, when out, from racing (4)
28. Nothing in their predator gets at what sheep provide (7)

Jigsaw No. 38 – PERIMETRICAL

Jigsaw No. 39 – PERIMETRICAL

Perimeter: The weight of 1 cubic foot of water, contrary to science, backed my fake: fake rich onyx tint is named after Austria's chocolate city (6: 8,2, 6-3,2,1).

1. Freudian historian with an audience (7)
2. Oxford companion takes wood without leave (7)
3. Feudal knight gets a girl in a cap (8)
4. Unruffled feathers? Take it easy! (4,4)
5. Low rank of officer for flag vessel? (10)
6. Drink some paraffin oil (4)
7. Jackal chronicler takes motor boat in river (7)
8. Terrible thing, suède: I'll drink to that! (10)
9. Harriet – nearly half of her's the opposite sex (6)
10. Home and not at home, to some extent (2,1,3)
11. Rand coin in exchange for mealies (6,4)
12. Gen – see under 'love' (4)
13. Feudal relationship of Goldie and me? (8)
14. Strand in the shade (6)
15. Sodium for a fellow who got leprosy (6)
16. Decree for one with wrongdoing coming up (4)
17. O for a new annual relating to part of speech (6)
18. Royal house as it used to be across the park (3,7)
19. Less than ladies and more than gents, and it shows (4)
20. Second note before first – repeat performance (4)
21. Go on horse and take its course (4)
22. Old English scholar with musical instrument inclined to sin (8)
23. Broadcasts from Genesis 500? (8)
24. Funks feast, funnily, and uses tobacco (5,5)
25. Resurrection time had dirty results (5,3)
26. Persons unknown with viruses (1-6)
27. Agreement about friend returning to address the Pantheon (2,4)
28. You reported a German customs union (10)

Jigsaw No. 39 – PERIMETRICAL

Jigsaw No. 40 – PERIMETRICAL

Perimeter: Rupert Brooke's heart after purification, we are asked to think (1,5,2,3,7,4,2,4).

1. Naval call from one Orcadian isle (4)
2. Sweet beast eats painter (7)
3. Tackle nosh when afflicted by a bit of gout, perhaps (10)
4. Dating letters, Roman and English, in unction characteristic of poet (10)
5. Foolish little flower? (4)
6. Barrier to Pole to get lost? (4)
7. Move slowly to the border (4)
8. Polisher Dick takes to clerical profession (that would be awful) (5-5)
9. Place in 'Butch Cassidy', with acknowledgement (4)
10. Just beautiful? So-so (4)
11. Girl, French one? Precisely (4)
12. Setter's to continue regardless, holding one mark (10)
13. Prisoner, drinking wine endlessly, can't manage stile (4,3)
14. Bargees have a legal right, outside Ghana, to time at school (10)
15. One who drives the island crazy? (7)
16. Juicy drinker (4)
17. The wife and Mo Mowly must be involved (2,3,5)
18. Name Aeroflot's changed – you can't have it! (3,3,4)
19. Evens or otherwise (4)
20. What's of value without a right is liable to be lost (10)
21. Divorce valley? (4)
22. Semi-thick type takes whisky on board (5,5)
23. It's used with pencil, etc, not too hard, held by South American idiot (6-4)
24. Coincidence in the kitchen, say? (4)
25. Apart from errors, the old black's about, darling … (10)
26. … in other words, child's confection with pastry (7-3)
27. Difficult problem – I'm disgusted – one digit out (7)
28. Poisonous tree makes you pass part (4)

Jigsaw No. 40 – PERIMETRICAL

Jigsaw No. 41 – PERIMETRICAL

The perimeter would be illegitimately christened, disturbing Brasenose College matron and fan (6,2,5,3,5,7).

1. Grecian urns as a measure of current hours (8)
2. A couple of beasts in a 5 (7)
3. Presently resembling the perimeter? (4)
4. Robin's adversary, perhaps, making hay of ear and stubble (10)
5. This is a hint about a disciple (4)
6. Number on short wave is disabled (7)
7. Free composition of Elgar – étude (10)
8. Arab chieftain holding the line with mush, which will smooth things over (5-5)
9. Liberal disarray among the enemy shows weakness (6)
10. Opportunities for discussion of different artists (4)
11. Fast mover has the cheek to give work to the queen (8)
12. Twenty winks? An indefinite number – maybe of eggs (4,1,5)
13. Home, Dario, to obtain data (4)
14. Stop vacation getting cancelled (5,3)
15. 2 in 2 of Mailer concerned with running a business (10)
16. Pole before and during part of opera in story-book realm (6)
17. Afraid to tender for one show (4)
18. Begin to ring London up, straight from the battery? (3-4)
19. Nyctalopic: 'If it is your bath —, please do pull down the —' (5-5)
20. Away with a Midland ruler (4)
21. Friend's about right: one in Birmingham's a disgrace (10)
22. No shillings and sixpence for a poet (4)
23. God – the Godhead – must be suffered (4)
24. Having several terms – parrot with nothing to eat talking (10)
25. A share in the Sun? Not I, not so! (6)
26. Scottish mouse is to settle itself eating Welsh vegetable (7)
27. Railway after Beeching? Mini-sell required (4,4)
28. Blunted warning? (3-3)

Jigsaw No. 41 – PERIMETRICAL

Jigsaw No. 42 – PERIMETRICAL

Perimeter: Musicians performing: everyone's looking forward to 'Tree weeder' and her Treen ware. (A 15 quote; other versions use the same words but not in this order.) (7,3,4,2,3,5,4)

1. Fly me first class both ways without cover (3,5)
2. Jumbles stories of people with weights (8)
3. Capital way to spell AS (6)
4. Thrash grain for girlfriend of writer of … (8)
5. … Buffalo Bill, taking in the first person … (6)
6. … by guess or by God? (6)
7. Unrelieved study of poet (6)
8. Waste place of the French politician (4)
9. Test team + (6,4)
10. He slept improperly with a Scottish girl (7)
11. Assessment of damage to main site (10)
12. Volcanic eruption in canteen – roof taken away (6)
13. Sweet donkey (4)
14. Multistorey accommodation for other than lodger? (5,5)
15. Like part of 6 5, H-Havelock's given his head (7)
16. What other way could you listen to a Welsh composer? (3,4)
17. Nightly display to a Welsh composer (4,4)
18. Dish of lamb in front – back before rainstorm (7)
19. Number 1 of 10 turns measuring three yards (4-4)
20. Nonpareil would make 9 8 (3-3)
21. What the arrogant put, where adulterers have bit (6)
22. Love to poet (French, not English) is smothered (8)
23. Part of 6 5 is in the exhibition (8)
24. The other (original) part of 6 5 loses its notes and gains two others separately in USA (6,4)
25. Old point or moment, not cup of woe (6)
26. Musical grass to which ungulates return (4)
27. Hamlet's silence or sleep (4)
28. Ear-rings? (8)

Jigsaw No. 42 – PERIMETRICAL

Jigsaw No. 43 – PERIMETRICAL

Perimeter: Tears are idle: poor Tim among evacuees from city gets £1000 (2,2,2,3,6,4,5,4).

1. St Francis's confession of folly? (6)
2. Thatcher's palm is a source of water (4)
3. From first to last it's love against the sea (4)
4. Italian mount loses heart in place of gambling (6)
5. 'Turn back, O man', surrounded by a number at home each way: it's spicy (10)
6. He carried cabbage night and day, as he put it (4,6)
7. Familiar name of 6's fish? (4)
8. Behaves like Bill Owen with rights? (8)
9. Bird and ass nearly meet in pub with royal associations (5,3)
10. Scots boy gets the sea-nymph (6)
11. Bird is following first and second (4)
12. Doing what romantics do, I'm both a businessman and a vocalist (10)
13. Small space with extraordinary secret in it (10)
14. Misleading piece of land (4)
15. Western sailor in South-Eastern stately home is not necessarily a stranger (8)
16. Not fluently written, perhaps with nothing durable? (8)
17. Tear with tightener and tear with loosener (8)
18. Greek island producing melons (6)
19. Fell into the grinder – give it a different name (7)
20. Loch Annan in a storm – time to be airily indifferent (10)
21. Maybe yellow, maybe rose – ouch! (8)
22. The gold at church is a flower (6)
23. See about a boy in the path of the ships (3-4)
24. Barman finds a way to come in lighter (7)
25. I'm 24, one way to keep sportspeople going (4,6)
26. Libel to get publicity during armistice (7)
27. Gemini – one and some more – with some conscience? (6)
28. Wales abandoning part of its university in Scotland (4)

Jigsaw No. 43 – PERIMETRICAL

Jigsaw No. 44 – PERIMETRICAL

The perimeter states that wild justice (Bacon) should be like salad –
shoved dried cress in with vegetables to make it (7,2,1,4,4,6,4).

1. God seems a first-class fellow (6)
2. Granny has an establishment with a psychological problem (10)
3. Love would get submerged in a footballer: most like brass (7)
4. Dog in the mouth (6)
5,13. Lettuce for baby with only one name, not quite complete – typical female behaviour! (4,3,5)
6. Smallholder upset rector, fathead at heart (7)
7. Mother goes to the races: Brother Lawrence risked twenty-nine distinct ones (10)
8. Study a heretic with old money (8)
9. Journalist entertaining composer made money (6)
10. A Western is showing; I can hear what's said (3-7)
11. It isn't bleached in the crude sense (4)
12. Mouth a kind of English? (7)
13. See 5
14. On one's way round in a trap with a complaint (5,3)
15. Criminal writer left to tell about chief starter (4,6)
16. Twin set, perhaps, English, with glutinous effect (6,4)
17. A bar to war? (4)
18. Dress on men could be the latest style (10)
19. The unpleasantness of Condé (4)
20. Information from every quarter (4)
21. First coming in, no longer fresh, it's smelly (4)
22. Sapper and doctor could be divorced here (4)
23. Hurt pet in outbuilding (7)
24. Shot with dagger? (4)
25. Girl to say nothing about American Indian coin (8)
26. Most of the adjoining houses have extravagant article as statuary material (10)
27. Covert operation to detect computing sequence (6)
28. Grape producer's way with police presence? (4,6)

Jigsaw No. 44 – PERIMETRICAL

Jigsaw No. 45 – PERIMETRICAL

Perimeter: Jeeves aims to accept a duelling challenge (1,9,2,4,12).

1. God-help-us time, especially when horrorstruck with no H about (4,4)
2. Assemblies following some of Python team in mathematics (6)
3. Snake in agony with tail cut off (6)
4. Successive notes on warden-led precautions for food at No 10 (8)
5. One ounce to take back from dog (6)
6. Ball to be fired, hitting the other two (6-4)
7. Person at bridge died, eaten by fish, one producing eggs (4,6)
8. Cinnamon takes in start of eye-opener heard from Northern stars (10)
9. Fight against international engagement (7)
10. Papa entertains famous actor, the cowardly fellow (7)
11. Flag officer? (6)
12. Hear Papa on broadcast using a rhetorical device (10)
13. Cine-addict to free me of girl (4-4)
14. Apologies: or is army responsible? (1,2,5)
15. I fled the country (4)
16. Horse with a snake (4)
17. The land of Lewis, an island backed outside Ulster (6)
18. Tincture of lemon as sauce in the Bahamas (6)
19. Yawning? There's nothing inadequate about it (8)
20. Acquisition of title that can be exploded (5,3)
21. Smoked beef – old mutton first (8)
22. Drink up, keeping first of beers for the locals (4)
23. Dissident Soviet scientist upset by a shark with a lot of eggs (8)
24. French writer's art reveals meat's off (6)
25. Middle name of Mobutu, the Home Counties knock-out (4)
26. Locum time for painting medium (7)
27. Drum may not play without piano (7)
28. Time off during fight with animation (6)

Jigsaw No. 46 – PERIMETRICAL

Perimeter: One humped beast first at gardens – awfully darn late first at gardens – has colour no. 6 in the Rubaiyat (1,4,4,5,3,4,4,1,2).

1. Pneumatic tire burst, keeping capital in account (10)
2. Expose falsehood in Scottish castle (6)
3. Song about outsider in pastoral setting (7)
4. Well off Scots make the most of life (4)
5. More or less an artist? Yes, with nothing on inside (10)
6. Bunting for 5 Ronald, we hear (4)
7. The company exulted (4)
8. Peggy – game old woman – follows original woman in church (8)
9. Any deer loose in Church house? (7)
10. No booze in room of one imprisoned for battery? (3-4)
11. Old priest backed farceur as life-giver (6)
12. More requested before sergeant comes in (6)
13. Volcano in Vietnam (4)
14. Disembowel above creatures for King George on a l-lake (8)
15. The first American car that crashed (6)
16. I go to sleep, little boy, briefly not without desire (10)
17. Violate, not without the border (8)
18. American soldier is in an arrangement for official emblems (8)
19. Where was Noah when the light went out? (2,3,3)
20. Scots town producing Irish grapes? (6)
21. Little Irish person given lunch with a peer (10)
22. Tea with honey surrounding an angel? (7)
23. Soft part of one's heart (4)
24. Little boy breaking one leg (6)
25. Liquor consumed after corporal punishment? (5-5)
26. Mystic in the Rubaiyat is enough to be heard in Paris, possibly (4)
27. Badly frightened by mistake in Diet's scheme (10)
28. Dress worn by Gulf characters, which isn't legal (8)

Jigsaw No. 46 – PERIMETRICAL

Jigsaw No. 47 – PERIMETRICAL

Perimeter: Oh, Oh, Oh, she's not your lady friend (3,4,1,3,3,4,2,8).

1. Points of view solvers backed and Telford attained (8)
2. Order to part? Not absolutely (6,4)
3. Draw his head and the rest on top (4)
4. Posh note in time to find Miss Welty (6)
5. Stage direction for team with alien exterior (4)
6. Note high ground that is a guide to sportsmen (7)
7. Skilled in making a sticky mess on inadequate data (4,2)
8. Say Hi! to one's beloved with waterweed (7)
9. I live the way of the ancient Swiss (8)
10. Eagles' short holiday terminated by Judith (10)
11. Inconsistent blow in all bedrooms? (3,3,4)
12. Jerome's self-portrait could be well foiled (4,6)
13. I'm going to pay Heather for spite (3-7)
14. They say PE for a bird is insulting to a black (3,4)
15. Chinese distance no distance from being one-dimensional (6)
16. Poet known as Ovid to some (4)
17. Susan with a break around Wiesbaden (6)
18. Solicitors forbidden? Finger stays down (3,3)
19. Funny to find a patient man doing casual labour (3,3)
20. Girl getting out of gaol (4)
21. Frank playwright who received five orange pips (8)
22. Obvious he's English, one going to Skye? (4,3,3)
23. Bring up from behind (4)
24. Dicky state of tree in Southern sea (8)
25. Elizabethan composer's height about six feet? (7)
26. Beat at the entrance of India's first Indian? (8)
27. Spooner's goal the gallery, where traveller must pay (4-4)
28. Refusal of custom (4)

Jigsaw No. 47 – PERIMETRICAL

Jigsaw No. 48 – PERIMETRICAL

Perimeter with 14: The King's singers, a dainty surprise (4,3,6,10,5,2,1,3).

1. Help on a horse? (4)
2. Not 'the warm South', dissolved in cataract (10)
3. A religious nobleman hasn't love but has hives (8)
4. Ceremony in Buenos Aires at a glance (8)
5. Nobleman aforesaid keeps love and becomes a poet (7)
6. Light wood on monk's head – it could be friar's (6)
7. Advisers to citizens utter where to find transport (3-4)
8. Make a bogy of a Scotsman on islands in river (8)
9. Corgi, deaf 'n' disorderly, on sale from me? (3-7)
10. Feathers not raised? (4)
11. Spurs food? (4)
12. Poor visibility for soldier at a town in Italy (6)
13. Put the bird in the oven, but I won't say grace (7)
14. See perimeter
15. Emetic formed from the ice-cap (6)
16. Writing-case in the desert abandoned by Hari and damn the consequences? (8)
17. Right-wing politicians smear balcony with mud (6,4)
18. Jimmy will fix it (4)
19. Not the busy times of dubiously safe children (3,7)
20. Prisoner about to cry after beer in the shade (4,6)
21. Did I manage the Queen? (4)
22. Seek to get hold of fragments of her car (5,3)
23. Groovy act of piracy? (7)
24. Having had a birth that was difficult per se, like the beetle in Gray's elegy (5-5)
25. Wrong, in part as in full (6)
26. Live on the way up into the grave – is it ticking away? (4-4)
27. Award for political achievement? (4)
28. Long John Silver's turn to pinch journalist (6)

Jigsaw No. 49 – PERIMETRICAL

Perimeter: 8's end – we hope – for which both fights fashioned roads home (3,5,2,3,6,3,3,3).

1. Wine tasting? Not altogether (4)
2. Take stand for the first time on the river (6)
3. Temptation coming by second entry to be in loco parentis (4-3)
4. Stoker keeping this month or having a moment of madness (10)
5. She was idle with a willow in her hand (4)
6. Drug that is treatment for those crazed with grief (10)
7. Enthusiasm for English (Irish?) absurdity, not Scottish leaders' science (10)
8. 'A poet could not but be gay' if he lost his right (4)
9. Jan abandons lower caste spy (4)
10. Plain or puzzling fellow among the saints? (6)
11. As plain as could be: I had one on top – possible top – of the building (5-5)
12. Lest males model, here's a covering in the window (10)
13. Top person's language bears fruit (8)
14. Organisation needed in the sanatorium (4)
15. Sickly pale, in love with film star Charles – he's in the wind (4,6)
16. It's a heavy blow where divorce comes up (4)
17. Zero food, just talk and talk? (8)
18. Conference, perhaps, or two, did you say? (4)
19. Correct neckwear has maybe 10 characteristics (10)
20. Throw up 'The Madness of King George'? (7)
21. Self-righteous becomes topless and wanton (7)
22. Will in person (4)
23. Composer came across in sanatorium first (7)
24. Inverted slabs display lichen, with beast eating 16 (8)
25. Most of the class have streaky hair? (6)
26. Unlucky day for hitter, then? (10)
27. Doctor in a row when something's been dropped (6)
28. Opera, half not the real thing at all, with warrantors on holiday? (8)

Jigsaw No. 49 – PERIMETRICAL

Jigsaw No. 50 – PERIMETRICAL (Variant)

The perimeter repeatedly displays the constituents of a rose when you …

1,16. … go round the railway junction (7,6)
2. Poe composed with guile the last words (8)
3. Shakespeare's word to avoid a musical by Lawrence (7)
4. One of exceptional brain using English letters (6)
5. Openings of homes are uncommon in Zimbabwe (6)
6. Greek orator makes Cleopatra's attendant eat milk pudding (8)
7. Some Christmas questions for such as Comus (6)
8. The hub of the church? (4)
9. Stairs may be a requirement outside their situation (8)
10. Subject of bulletin on 'oliday's given Peruvian currency (3,4)
11. Black bat and black bird, possibly having rent (5-5)
12. Aunt in Mansfield Park gives name to root for perfumery (6)
13. Desire missing more or less at the present moment (6)
14. Good food supplies rent unit (8)
15. Transporter of liquid or work, perhaps, makes the odd pile in a tree (8)
16. See 1
17. Post Office writing to Brits in Oz (4)
18. Pirate to seem odd (4)
19. Long-term plans to place rodent, say, in pigs' homes (10)
20. He gets surprisingly thronged about: no fun to be dragged through it (5-5)
21. Hardy girl holds dance: like the steppe? (8)
22. Bringer of food is confused with waters (8)
23. Insect used to be quiet (4)
24. Merchant seaman following awkward situation, reportedly (10)
25. Keys, perhaps, for cockney lights (7)
26. Engineers in crafty tricks at beginning of steam radio (8)
27. It's authorised in an RAF unit in Surrey (6)
28. Launcher of spear for endless females with guns (6)

Jigsaw No. 50 – PERIMETRICAL (Variant)

Jigsaw No. 51 – PERIMETRICAL

Perimeter: A cynical saying: — Impossible! Not even Kipling's Danny, twisted to begin with in personality, takes English newspaper when Ulster's pushed around (2,4,4,4,4,11).

1. Victim of the perimeter backed teashop between two hills (10)
2. Awaken heavenly body with exposure of lie (4,2,4)
3. With the majority inside a doss-house (4)
4. Renounce hell in favour of a form of heraldry (10)
5. Reduces the money stevedores get, for God's sake, with chemical warfare? (5,5)
6. Wyatt of the Listener's page (4)
7. Stick back cover on geometry book (6)
8. Doggone! All you need to finish the game (6,4)
9. German has captured Pole (4)
10. Fancy one with silver in its source? (7)
11. A pound for setter in this month's payment (10)
12. A room to suit? (6)
13. Modern liturgy reportedly is a painful thing (8)
14. Inn laid out for building by birds (10)
15. Author of 'A Yellow Christmas'? (4,6)
16. Overs by Dexter show strength of field (7)
17. 15th and 7th shaped like 19th (4)
18. It's precious to love a friend (4)
19. Very big call to see capital (4)
20. Slavish follower putting in for race at White City? (7,3)
21. Adds something to Thomson's poem (7)
22. Author of 'Yes But No' sounds French (7)
23. Wide boy takes great men aback (4)
24. Very loud gun moved into Royal Artillery (10)
25. Keep end of fruit drinks for fencing (8)
26. Forbidden bill for upper class (4)
27. A French company too Scottish? (4)
28. Major stars of our salvation (4)

Jigsaw No. 51 – PERIMETRICAL

Jigsaw No. 52 – PERIMETRICAL

Perimeter: A stormy night in the castle (chessboard piece): it 21 (a song) (1,11, ... 2,8,6).

1. Burns's Jo with vulgar kid? (8)
2. Prestigious employment, acquired by Horner's pull, for patient man (1,4,3)
3. Nod – in the way it was dispatched (6)
4. Moulding stars young female (8)
5. More or less half the dance circle (5)
6. Stage direction in Romeo & Juliet: return seen arranged (5,5)
7. English opening for sporting contest? (5)
8. Jokes Ginger contrived stink, giving occasion for tug of war (5,5,5)
9. Agitated about article to make rechauffé (4,2)
10. Tom Ellis's lead part in Macbeth (6)
11. It's blown at the Cape (4)
12. He has stocks in cloth of gold, perhaps (8)
13. Club's first – club's first, as fate would have it (6)
14. Poor Jo in a cap bearing quinces (8)
15. Bartholomew, for example, turned morning to evening and a king to a queen (3,5)
16. Sewer evokes hostility (6)
17. See 24
18. Footballer accepts work from his relations (6)
19. Couches for pastries entered by model (8)
20. Study concerned with publicity (4)
21. Celebrated Norman blood? (4)
22. Where philosophy was taught in Athens to Athenians (4)
23. Start of month: later we turn and gaze vacantly (3,3,4)
24,17. What's in an hour-glass? We can leave our footprints there (3,5,2,4)
25. The first volume of Ovid's exile (4)
26. Brunette princess's Mass book – sue for it (6,9)
27. Vulgar search for herb? No (6)
28. That's tasty! First train leaves at 3.10 (4)

Jigsaw No. 52 – PERIMETRICAL

Jigsaw No. 53 – PERIMETRICAL

Around the perimeter, clockwise from the top left-hand corner, goes what happened to a grandfather clock (28 17 5 indicates the time) (2,7,5,5,2,2,5).

1. The hairstyle gives one away (4)
2. Man losing head at fall of (say) USSR leader (8)
3. Villa I abandoned in amazement (10)
4. Note: between front and sides of head are beasts (5,5)
5. Performed without direction and faded away (4)
6. I make pictures of old, if I must (4,6)
7. Scots leave off British political quartet (4,2,4)
8. Gypsy enters giving it an answer (6)
9. Note: abandoned queen wants Richard III (7)
10. Big guns of value to town of literary fame (7)
11. A risky cricket stroke means the end of the pirate captain (4,4)
12. Scots name for two parts of India (4)
13. King Mark's largely a familiar name in a 6 (6)
14. Where the ball is invisible and possibly is much rent (2,3,5)
15. Australian fast bowler does badly in general (6)
16. One right in the head finds theology somewhere in the New Testament (8)
17. Familiar term of address for a fellow from Hoy or Coniston (3,3)
18. Wanting a male, not a chance without one (2,4)
19. St. Mary the Virgin, Oxford? That hurt! (4)
20. Where the French go to join the unemployed (3,2,3)
21. Writer and space traveller thought to have got through (10)
22. Promise to find a quiet shelf (6)
23. I used to be aware, now I'm prudent (8)
24. Feeling chronic pain among heavyweights that move impossibly fast (8)
25. Free hot concoction brings its old usage (7)
26. Fuss at foxhole? (2-2)
27. Unaccompanied coupon between town and river (4)

28,17,5. See preamble (4,3,3,3,4)

Jigsaw No. 53 – PERIMETRICAL

Jigsaw No. 54 – PERIMETRICAL (Variant)

The top and bottom lines of the perimeter, read across, and the left and right sides, read down, consist of: — Time for the nods of a fireside reader (4 [you are] 3,3,4,3,4,2,5).*

1. Charge card taking coppers in (6)
2. A harvest home? Not me: I've some bias towards keeping my feet on the ground (10)
3. Jolly good hot drink for a dog (8)
4. Hurry to get a bribe (4)
5. In d-dubious surroundings I find religion a problem (10)
6. Debtor to order 10 for identical servant (6)
7. They are cold, and the festival is false (10)
8. Old oath signifying the energy to fish? (4)
9. Jumper takes part of water plant (7)
10. Urchin, ex-road-hog (according to the old jest) (8)
11. Alice's caterpillar was exactly three, put into office (7)
12. Desire a Manx cat? Put an offer in (6)
13. Bird resembling extra-terrestrial holds gold (8)
14. From which one can only come up and see Mae? (6)
15. Successful businessman from Rome, key man with a difference (10)
16. Use or ornament? One below's around (7)
17. Hard sweet converted to a gun (6)
18. Concert halls were for poetry first (4)
19. Whence comes the heavenly hunter accepting US soldier for nothing (6)
20. Past pas? The mark may be next (8)
21. Margaret keeps wreck of boat in rural Irish setting (4,3)
22. Joint problem for heart and music, possibly (10)
23. Possible limit to English island (4)
24. Salmon poacher every year starts a dance in its valley (4)
25. Fish here with container, likely to form a precedent (4,4)
26. What I get from the deal is fated for destruction (5-3)
27. Saint-Exupery's part – restraining the composer – requires padding etc. (10)
28. Lush is a loser (4)

*The spelling of one word in the perimeter is different in different editions; I have preferred the usual English spelling which however is NOT that used in the *Oxford Dictionary of Quotations*.

Jigsaw No. 54 – PERIMETRICAL (Variant)

Jigsaw No. 55 – PERIMETRICAL

Clue for the perimeter and 17: The back to back Mlle de Beauvoir embraces, madly if lonely, the French boys: study is more appropriate than regret (5,3,2,8,2,4,4,7).

1. One people? Not according to nonconformists (4)
2. The golden cherry makes the stables dirty (6)
3. Madagascan beast accepting an order (3-3)
4. Provide money for bread at the water's edge (8)
5. Break … saucer? (6)
6. Posthumously provided with the MBE and another medal? (8)
7. What may happen to a Czech, say, or a Pole, in an endless Manchester riot (10)
8. Admittance after the soup? (6)
9. Accompaniment to 'Round the Horn' is French (6)
10. Country music becomes a habit, keeping all right without line (4,4)
11. Frenchman carrying a weapon? (4)
12. State may fruit with first eleven? (6)
13. Female at Queens, an obstructive one (8)
14. Insect to make live-in solvers sharp? (5-3)
15. One left nothing in Latin, is the inference (8)
16. He works in a custom-house, the solid one among the liquid (4-6)
17. Education diminishes when there's an audience (7)
18. I'm thinking about it – one step enough, said Newman? (3,2,3)
19. Places for a genius? (4)
20. It's pretty high: was it Portia's seat, near Vicenza? (10)
21. Warm or close to the left (4)
22. Doubter inclined to stick out (7)
23. … and young lax? (3,4)
24. Ordained Queen almost becomes a merry-maker (8)
25. Astringent for your hat, a nylon extract (7)
26. So far the fox has consumed … (2,4)
27. Use a needle when backing sorters' arrangement in Scotland (6,4)
28. A discipline for soldiers in a Jewish day (6)

Jigsaw No. 55 – PERIMETRICAL

Jigsaw No. 56 – PERIMETRICAL

Perimeter: I finished the weekend worth less, sadly, with 3 to come, mated by mates, I'd say (4,7,4,5,3,5,[7]).

1. Not being 3 with Leicester? (8)
2. Dismal and uninteresting, without a listener (6)
3. Times? (7)
4. Bizarre sect keeping anthropoids in the watch (10)
5. Amount of work left among dodges in Florida (10)
6. Spooner's quarrel with Sylvia as to where the plane should go (6,4)
7. Part exchange other malodorous objects like geysers (10)
8. Rudolf or Myra hold a service in which Macbeth died (see Act 5 Scene 1) (7)
9. Drawer with varied hue and rail (7)
10. I agree what to do with both ears (4,4)
11. I have a jazz piece for an audience: I form the frozen steps (3-3)
12. Home expert at a pow-wow (6)
13. Berry found round here according to the French reasoner (8)
14. Think back on one's share of praise etc. (4)
15. No tricks relating to Scrooge before a penitential psalm (8)
16. Italian city in Italian siesta, perhaps, with oil producer (6)
17. Don't stop talking for grub (4)
18. Common sense for the British abroad (4)
19. Ascending, we have the fourth number displayed (2,4)
20. Past actors under a cloud? (8)
21. Upset or otherwise in attitude (7)
22. Stock farmer managed with monarch in prison (8)
23. Noise made by journalists? (6)
24. A scheme in the diocese easily ditched? (8)
25. Star attributed to Susie? (6)
26. Psychotherapist's contract (6)
27. Dog carrying things? (4)
28. Abusive epithet such as 'shower' turned on (8)

Jigsaw No. 56 – PERIMETRICAL

Jigsaw No. 57 – PERIMETRICAL (Variant)

Doctor Faustus gives the reason for his choice of dwelling: '10 12 18'
followed by the perimeter (read clockwise from a point to be determined on
the left-hand side of the diagram) which might be rendered 'Harass'd an'
lost, destination hell' (3,3,2,5,4,2,3,6).

1.	Coming 5 during a depression	(6)
2.	Help without direction in a poem	(6)
3.	Consign to limbo, perhaps, from most of 9-burg	(8)
4.	Fishy affairs, as in song	(7)
5.	Infidel found at burglary	(7)
6.	Whistle-blowing from French and Latin about love	(8)
7.	Peace people's place where Italy's on the side of the French	(8)
8.	Interval arranged at centre	(8)
9.	Part of island, one of three on river	(6)
10,12,18.	Be sick at decree 'The self must be curtailed in small bites' – see preamble	(6,2,2,5,4)
11.	Jinx on academic wear? You surprise me!	(6)
12.	See 10	
13.	A shrub for a king (am I wrong?) at first	(6)
14.	Missing link in the oven	(4)
15.	Girl that is – that was – no bitch!	(6)
16.	Class with fewer clothes?	(6)
17.	Young queen left sick, for my money	(8)
18.	See 10	
19.	Head American with old shirt	(6)
20.	Having a psychological problem to counter, I need treatment	(8)
21.	Dutch Beatrix?	(5,3)
22.	Anagram, perhaps – what was that? – in spots	(6)
23.	King states his view on society's dicky state	(8)
24.	Surgeon looked at individuals in middle management	(8)
25.	This bird was the rare variety	(10)
26.	He is, I'm inclined to reveal, the man who cursed David	(6)
27.	Six-nickel amalgam from authentic try to extract gold	(6-4)
28.	He painted his own bird	(7)

Jigsaw No. 57 – PERIMETRICAL (Variant)

Jigsaw No. 58 – PERIMETRICAL (Variant)

Perimeter: The top and right-hand side of the perimeter are a series of books (8,6) by the left-hand side and bottom (read down and across) (3,6,5).

1. Pay for an extra at cricket (4)
2. It's irregular to use clay (International Cricket Club) (7)
3. Change 1 across's opening time (4)
4. Row on a river, maybe with more craft too (6)
5. Pet with singular courage goes for strings (6)
6. Ancient Roman with nine tails? (4)
7. MCC's hot air sadly colours study (10)
8. See 18
9. Place where the 'girls are mean and dirty' has the same name (6)
10. The chelonian's level (7)
11. Tree ring on fire? (4)
12. Former partner's flower show (4)
13. I can't believe it, but lyric in bed baffles me (10)
14. Water where there should be oil: get angry about it (8)
15. Mourn for morn coming in fast (6)
16. Letters put on line by personality doing Cambridge exam (6,2)
17. Stew in the army coach, one I'm building (10)
18,8. Burlesque conclusion in which fate, in circles, leads valorous person to crude weapon (7,8)
19. Skilled at faking 'nice' in return (10)
20. Tear the Queen's feathers and put in the liquidiser? (6,4)
21. Terror-stricken outside church, call for attention from behind the high altar (10)
22. Actor Anthony takes wood for forest (4)
23. Pretty little pictures prepared for publication? (10)
24. Vessels of the fleet in America (4)
25. Most of the face must be shown on the passport (4)
26. Unsettled person? Stick to Queens (8)
27. Increase for Labour at Warwick Castle? (7)
28. Fared ill, being eaten by monster in Yorkshire (10)

Jigsaw No. 58 – PERIMETRICAL (Variant)

Jigsaw No. 59 – PERIMETRICAL (Variant)

The top and right-hand side of the perimeter form a book (8,6) by the left-hand side and bottom (read down and across) (7,7).

1. Do claim chops are cooked (10)
2. Dog with my German dish (4,4)
3. At the vicarage she may be in charge – we fry leg (6,4)
4. Meals pass for love among Mediterranean peoples (10)
5. Work among fish that played ball (10)
6. Juicy steak provides a sac (4)
7. Burner of cakes turning into Wyatt's attachments (8)
8. Birds – first to last there would be one of nine (4)
9. Eat and sleep here, solver, in surmise at the end (5-5)
10. Playwright's son makes fourth change from play (6)
11. Some encroachment into housework is better than battery (3,4)
12. Rash of bills following Peruvian note (10)
13. Birds, not female, incorporated males by narrow margin (6)
14. Smith's job on back row to be annoying outside (8)
15. Connection with royalty no good? (7)
16. French town of glass (4)
17. What the cow said is said making a face (4)
18. One in the masquerade 'The Silent Sea' in France (6)
19. Unauthorised retreat? (4)
20. Walker on carpet, in charge of pub at first, unlikely to get excited (10)
21. What defendant has to make sure to make happiness (4)
22. Leave no-one undisturbed in uninhabited island (7)
23. Footballers in costume after game? (6)
24. Heard extract from 'O si sic omnia!', sailing badly (7)
25. Visionary has backing of Welshman (4)
26. Smiles promoted correction of the flesh (English record) (4-4)
27. First-class bristle (4)
28. Best off with a sleet storm (10)

Jigsaw No. 59 – PERIMETRICAL (Variant)

Jigsaw No. 60 – PERIMETRICAL (Variant)

The top and bottom lines of the perimeter, read across, and the left and right sides, read down, are four sports beginning with the same letter; they are in alphabetical order.

1. I am in cot, possibly, but I was in this fluid (8)
2. A sleeping-bag has to be funny (3-4)
3. Name article in TV programme (6)
4. French statesman's clue, menace to solvers (10)
5. Business for former pupil, a non-starter, right? – looking like a pillar (8)
6. Little girl once in trouble (6)
7. Many discover the truth about a sweet (7)
8. Literally original element of society microscopically examined (6)
9. Direct from taking part which is difficult (8)
10. I leave the nest for Jane (4)
11. I reviewed Clift semi-criminally cast (4,6)
12. Provocatively show the flag to relative after pinching the silver (6)
13. Soldier's mood is surrender (4,2)
14. See virgins' problem? It's inhaled (10)
15. Bury old companions with medals, say (10)
16. What could be rosier, an instrument like Hamlet? (10)
17. Lament being sharp (4)
18. Fifty snakes and their opposites (7)
19. Student in love with artistic cut? (4)
20. Group of a thousand brains eating second starter (3-4)
21. Cash covering half the winter in California (8)
22. Vulgar piano allowed a group of notes (8)
23. Make over coloured ring (4)
24. Stand for light – don't talk vacation when the less polite are around (4-6)
25. Mystic providing America with backing (4)
26. The sea works its wheel: cultivate about half (8)
27. Bare hoof? Weed after sunset (6)
28. Employer's turn to serve beginners (4)

Jigsaw No. 60 – PERIMETRICAL (Variant)

Solutions

Jigsaw No. 1 – ALPHABETICAL

Plays by Oscar Wilde (Crow's ideal, anag) are AN IDEAL HUSBAND, THE IMPORTANCE OF BEING EARNEST, LADY WINDERMERE'S FAN, SALOME, A WOMAN OF NO IMPORTANCE

A. ALL/U/RED
B. BRASSED OFF (anag)
    BRIDE/WELL
C. CUM/IN
D. DE<LET>E
E. EARNEST (art, vb)
F. FORCE-FEED (anag)
G. GUM TREES
H. See I
I. (with H) I/DEAL/ H<USB>AND
    IMPORT/AN/CE
J. JOSH
K. KIDS WEAR (anag)
L,W,M. LAD<Y/ WIN>DER/MERE

M. See L: M/ONGREL (anag)
N. NASH/GAB
O. OLIGOCENE (anag)
P. PY<REX>IA (anag)
Q. QUARTERS
R. RES/INISED (anag)
S. S<A/L>OME
T. THE TA/LI/BAN
U. UNETH(ical)
V. VEN<ETIAN>ED
W. See L: W<OM>AN
X. (vi)XEN/URINE
Y. YO<U>-ALL (anag)
Z. Z/END

Jigsaw No. 2 – ALPHABETICAL

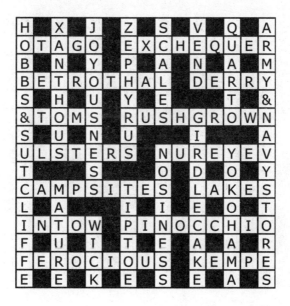

A. ARMY & NAVY STORES
B. BET/ROT/HAL
C. C<A/MP' S>ITES
D& DERRY/ &/ TOMS
E. EX/CHEQUER
F. FEROC/IOUS
G. GIRDLE CAKE
H. HOBBS & SUTCLIFFE (anag)
I. IN TO/W
J. JO<YOU/S/N/E>SS
K. KEMPE (anag)
L. LAKES
M. MATURE (hidden)
N. NO<SINES>S: NUR/EYE/V

O. O<TAG>O
P. PIN/OCCHIO
Q. QUART/O
R. RUSH-/GROWN
S. SCALES
T. TI<PTO>E
U. ULSTERS (anag)
V. V/END
W. WICK
X. X/AN<THOU>S
Y. YOKOHAMA (anag)
Z. ZE<P/H/Y/R>US
&   See D

Jigsaw No. 3 – ITALIAN ALPHABETICAL

A. ACIERATES (hidden)
   ALPS
B. B<LESSING>S
   BOTH SIDES
C. C/OLD
   C<OTT>AGE
D. DE<D>ANS
E. END/U/E
F. FILLE D/E <CHAM/B>RE
G. GNAT (rev)
H. HAN<DINES>S: HATP/IN
I. IT/A/LIAN A/L/PH/A/BET

L. LE/COQ
M. MISDONE (anag): MOVING
N. NITRO-DERIVATIVE (anag)
O. OUT/POST
P. PHINEAS F(inn)/ LETCHER
Q. QUENTIN (hidden)
R. RUE/LLI/A
S. SPLIT(t) IN'/F<IN/IT>IVE
T. THREADS (anag)
U. (s)URGE ON
V. VALET/U/DINAR/IAN
Z. ZEUS (Suez)

Jigsaw No. 4 – GREEK ALPHABETICAL

	P	O	S	P		O	A	L

A. A<RIS/TO/C>/RAT
B. BIEN/NIAL
G. GALEN/A
D. DE <SOT>O
E (short). E/STATESMEN (anag)
Z. ZOO<THE/CI/U>M
E (long). EAT LUNCH (anag)
TH. THE TA/BL<OID PR>ESS
I. I/DEAL/I/ST
K. KNEE
L. LEATHER SUITCASE (anag)
M. MOTH-ER

N. NI/SSEN (rev)
X. XER/XES (rev)
O(short). O/X/I/DI<S>ED
P. PLANE/TIC
R. RO<OM/S TO LE>T
S. SETTER
T. TAIL(or)
U. UGLY
PH. PHILANTHROPICAL (anag)
CH. CHAMBERS
PS. PSYCHOSOMIMETIC (anag)
O(long). OMEN (hidden)

Jigsaw No. 5 – ALPHABETICAL with a difference

	A	B	C	D	E	F	G
H	E	L	I	O	Z	O	A	I	B	A	D	A	N
	R	Q	A	W	G	W	S
J	A	G	U	A	R	K	O	H	I	N	O	O	R
	T	I		I	T		L
L	E	A	N	M	A	N	C	H	I	N	E	E	L
	T	O	S	O	E	N
O	P	T	I	O	N	S	Q	U	I	G	L	E	Y
E	L	O	R	R	A
S	P	E	E	C	H	L	E	S	S	T	O	U	T
T	Y	S	I	N
V	I	E	W	A	B	L	E	X	A	V	I	E	R
D	A	R	I	R	E	A
Y	E	H	U	D	I	Z	E	A	L	L	E	S	S
S	L	D	E	Y	Y	Y

1. I/BAD/AN	15. FAWN
2. A/ERA/T(im)E	16. HELIOZOA (anag)
3. KO<(r)HINO>OR	17. C<Z>AR
4. DAW/KINS	18. JAGUAR
5. PEP/TIDES	19. Q/UIGLEY (anag)
6. OPTIONS (anag)	20. RE-/SEIZE
7. MO/NO/HYBRID	21. SPEE(d)/CH<L>ESS
8. GA<SO>LEN/E	22. WAUL (Wall, MND)
9. MAN/CH/IN/EEL	23. X/AV<I>ER
10. X-/RAY	24. Y/EH/UDI (Menuhin)
11. TOUT	25. VI<EW/AB>LE
12. LE/AN	26. EIGHT H/OURS
13. NE<GATI>VELY (anags)	27. UNEASY
14. ZEALLESS (hidden)	28. B<IQUINTI(anag)>LE

128

Jigsaw No. 6 – APHORISTICAL

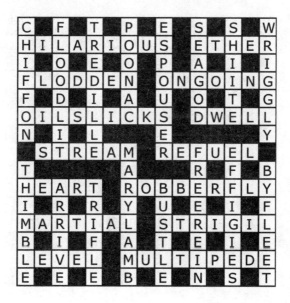

1. ARRIVE(derci)	16. MARY/ LAMB
2. BUSTLE	17. MUL<TIP/ED>E
3. BY/FLEET	18. OIL SLICKS
4. CHI<FFO>N	19. ON/GOING
5. D/WELL	20. POONA/C
6. EFFI<GI>E'S	21. REFU(s)E/L
7. ESPOUSER (anag)	22. RO/B/BER FLY (anag)
8. ETHER (hidden)	23. SE<A G>OD
9. FLO/DDEN (F. of the forest)	24. S<HI>ITE
10. FL<OODL(es)>IT	25. ST<R>EAM
11. FRE/E RE/IN	26. ST<RIG>IL
12. HE/ART	27. THIMBLE (hidden)
13. HILAR/IOUS	28. TRE<DILL>E
14. LEVEL	29. TRIFLE
15. MARTIAL (marshal)	30. W<RIGG>LY

Jigsaw No. 7 – APHORISTICAL

1.	ADAR (hidden)		19.	(t)O/BE/A/H(ome)
2.	ARE/A		20.	OR/AL
3.	A/RIA		21.	PLATONISE (anag)
4.	A/MA/T<O>RIAL		22.	RAIL T(anag)/RAVEL
5.	AUDIBLE (anag)		23.	RE(al)LY
6.	(BALL) See 27		24.	RILE(Ryle)
7.	BE/ST/ WI/SHES		25.	SCAR(y)
8.	CALM SEAS (anag)(same scal)		26.	S<NO>OP
9.	CAN'T		27,6.	SNOWBALL (see *Animal Farm*)
10.	CAR/B/ON		28.	SQUI<NT-E/YE>D
11.	C/OM/MON RO(via)/OM		29.	STAN/MORE (Bakerloo)
12.	CUR/D		30.	SWOTS (anag)
13.	EMENDATION (anag)		31.	TAEL (tale)
14.	EOCENE (anag)		32.	T/AWDRY
15.	HEART/BURN		33.	THE N/ATIVE (rev)
16.	LLA/NO (rev)		34.	TOOT/HB/RUSH
17.	NELL (hidden)		35.	VACUUM
18.	NUDE (anag)		36.	WA(te)RSHIP

Jigsaw No. 8 – APHORISTICAL

1.	A/GRIPPA	16.	ELEP/HANT(s)
2.	A/NUB/IS	17.	EVE/R
3.	ARIA (hidden)	18.	(pr)IM<IT>ATE
4.	ATTACHE	19.	MERR<Y> WIFE (anag)
5.	AT/TEST	20.	NUT/RIENT
6.	BARKE<EPE(e)>R	21.	OBLIGATED (anag)
7.	BAT/TERSE/A	22.	O/B(u)T/RUDE
8.	BERG	23.	ONE-STEP (hidden)
9.	C/RAVEN	24.	PARKIN/SON
10.	DIN/E	25.	PU<TRIDNE>SS
11.	DRESS COAT (anag)	26.	RAV<AG>ER
12.	E<AC>H	27.	S<HIP>WAY
13.	E<C>LAT (rev)	28.	SPLI<N>TS
14.	E/F/FETE	29.	TONNE (anag)
15.	(m)ELBA	30.	WIN/DOW' S/ASH

Jigsaw No. 9 – APHORISTICAL

B	A	C	K	S	T	A	Y	S		S	T	E	A	M
L		U		E		R		Q		H		N		O
A	E	R	A	T	E	D		U	G	A	N	D	A	N
S		A		T		O		I		M		O		E
T	A	C	T		S	U	R	G	E		B	R	A	Y
O		A		M		R		G		U		S		
F	L	O	R	A	L		B	L	O	N	D	E	L	L
F			L		O		Y		M					I
S	T	R	A	T	I	F	Y		P	A	T	H	A	N
		A		A		F		T		N		I		E
A	S	T	I		I	G	L	O	O		E	L	L	A
I		A		S		U		D		B		A		M
R	U	B	E	L	L	A		A	H	O	H	I	T	E
E		L		A		R		Y		N		R		N
D	R	E	A	M		D	I	S	I	N	V	E	S	T

1.	A<ERA>TED
2.	A/HO<HIT>E (2 Sam 23 9)
3.	AI/RED
4.	ARDOUR ('arder)
5.	A/ST/I
6.	BACK/STAYS
7.	B<LAST>-OFF(in)S
8.	BLONDE/LL
9.	BONN (bon, bonne)
10.	BRAY
11.	CU/RAC/A/O
12.	DI'S/IN/VEST
13.	D<RE>AM
14.	ELLA (hidden)
15.	EN<DOR>SE
16.	FLORAL (anag)
17.	HI<LAIR>E
18.	I/G<LO>O
19.	LINE<AM>ENT (anag)
20.	MAL/TA
21.	M<ONE>Y
22.	OFF GUARD
23.	PATH/AN
24.	RA/TABLE
25.	RUB/ELLA
26.	SETT(ers)
27.	(Peter)SHAM
28.	SLAM
29.	S<QUI(d)GG>LY
30.	S/TEAM
31.	STRA<TIF>Y
32.	S/URGE
33.	T/ACT
34.	TO<DA>YS
35.	UGANDAN (hidden)
36.	UN<MA>N

Jigsaw No. 10 – APHORISTICAL

S	N	O	W	D	R	I	F	T		R	I	G	H	T
A		D		E		C		I		E		R		O
I	M	I	T	A	T	E		R	E	P	L	I	C	A
L		S		L		B		E		O		S		S
B	Y	T	E			O	B	S	E	R	V	A	N	T
O			S		X		I		T		I			
A	B	B	A	C	Y		C	A	M	E	L	L	I	A
T		L		A		S		S		D		L		U
S	T	E	M	P	L	E	S		E	L	D	E	S	T
		M		E		M		S		Y				O
Z	E	I	T	G	E	I	S	T			G	A	E	L
E		S		R		O		A		A		V		A
B	Y	H	E	A	R	T		S	O	L	O	I	S	T
R		E		C		I		I		L		L		R
A	D	D	L	E		C	A	S	S	O	W	A	R	Y

1. (Eg)ABBAC/Y(alp) (rev) (plage)
2. ADDLE (anag)
3. 'ALL/O
4. AUTO/L/A/TRY
5. A<VI>LA
6. BLE<MI/SH>ED
7. BY HEART (anag)
8. BYTE (8 bits; bight)
9. CAME/LLI/A
10. C<ASS>O/WARY
11. DEAL
12. ELDEST (hidden)
13. GAE/L
14. GR<IS/A>ILLE
15. ICE/BOX
16. I'M/I/TATE

17. OBSERVANT (anag)
18. ODIST (hidden)
19. R<EP[L]IC>A
20. REP<OR/TED>LY
21. RIGHT
22. SA/I/L-B/OATS
23. SCA/PEG/RACE
24. SEMI<O>TIC
25. S<NOW/DR>IFT
26. SOL/OIST
27. STASIS
28. S/TEMPLES
29. TIRES/I/A/S
30. TOAST
31. ZE/BRA
32. ZE<ITGEI>ST

Jigsaw No. 11 – APHORISTICAL

1.	AB/RA(i)DED	16.	I/MP/OSE UPON (opus one)
2.	AG/ED	17.	IN THE FIRST PLACE
3.	(ch)AMBER	18.	LI<EG/E-LOR>DS
4.	A/PIARY (anag)	19.	M<ON>ARCH
5.	A<VIA>T/RIX	20.	OPRAH (Harpo)
6.	CRASH	21.	PASS DEGREE (not honours)
7.	DR/Y ROT	22.	P<(v)ICTORIA>L
8.	DU/N(b)/LIN	23.	PLE<CTR>A
9.	EMPTY ROOM (anag)	24.	RHINO (anag)
10.	ENEMIES (anag)	25.	RI/ALTO
11.	ES/CHEATED	26.	SHAM(e)
12.	GREY	27.	THEODOSIUS (anag)
13.	HIDE	28.	TRAVERS(e)
14.	HI/G<H ALT>AR(den)	29.	UNSPOILT (anag)
15.	HUMERUS		

Jigsaw No. 12 – APHORISTICAL

	R	B		D	N		K		O		A
P	R	I	V	A	T	E	A	U	D	I	E	N	C	E
I		V		C		M		M		S		S		O
S	P	E	C	K	L	Y		E	P	S	I	L	O	N
T		R		Y			R				O			
O	L	D	R	A	I	L	W	A	Y		S	W	A	P
L		E		R		A		T					L
E	V	E		D	E	B	R	I	E	F		F	E	U
E				O		O		L		R			U	M
R	O	B	E		F	U	N	N	Y	I	D	E	A	S
		O			R			N		E			T
S	O	P	R	A	N	I		C	U	T	I	C	L	E
H		E		L		T		O		I		I	O	A
O	V	E	R	S	P	E	C	I	A	L	I	S	E	D
O		P		O		S		L		Y			T

1. A/EON (one, one)
2. ALSO (hidden)
3. BACK/YARD (nimby)
4. BO-PEEP
5. COIL
6. CUTICLE (cue tickle)
7. DE<BRIE>F
8. (aca)DEMY (paper sizes)
9. EPS/ILON
10. EVE
11. FEU (Fr.)
12. FL<IN/TIL>Y
13. FREE-COST (anag)
14. FUNNY IDEAS (anag)
15. KISS (hidden) ('Kiss kiss')
16. LABOURITES (anag)
17. NUM/ERA/TION
18. OLD RAILWAY (anag)
19. ON/SLOW (Former MP; TV Keeping Up Appearances)
20. OVER/SPE<CIALIS>ED
21. PI<STOLE>ER
22. PLUM/STEAD
23. PRIVATE/ AUDIENCE
24. R/I/VER DE/E
25. R/OBE
26. SHOO (shoe)
27. SOP/RANI
28. S<PECK>LY
29. SWAP (paws)

135

1.	AC/ME	19.	I<NEP>T
2.	A/DD/END/A	20.	MAESTRO (anag)
3.	ANTE	21.	MA<RI>MBA
4.	A/PRON(e)	22.	MUIR
5.	A/SHE	23.	MU/LATTO (anag)
6.	A/STON<I>ED	24.	O/CELLAR
7.	A/W<N>ING	25.	O/'LD/ LAG
8.	BASRA (anag)	26.	ON/ A/HEAD
9.	B/LOTTO	27.	P<OIL>U
10.	B<ODG>ED	28.	P/ON/TIFF
11.	CON/SCRIPT	29.	RACK/-RAIL
12.	DEAR SIR (anag)	30.	ROAD MAP (anag)
13.	DEC(k)/ATHLON(e)	31.	ROOTS
14.	DI/SP<R>OOF	32.	SERPS (anag)
15.	EMOTION (anag)	33.	SH<ARP>ISH
16.	ENSA (hidden)	34.	S<QUACC>O
17.	E/T/U/I	35.	TEST
18.	GONER/I/L	36.	UN/DO

Jigsaw No. 14 – APHORISTICAL

1.	A/F(oo)T/ER	17.	K/AFF(a)IR
2.	AIDA/N	18.	NETT (anag)
3,23.	AM/OUR/ PROP/RE	19.	N<ORTH-W>EST
4.	AWASH (hidden)	20.	OBOLI (hidden)
5.	BARB (Barbara, Bob)	21.	OC/TAD
6.	BLYTH (blithe)	22.	POINTEDLY (anag)
7.	CAN<NON-AD>ES	23.	(PROPRE) See 3
8.	DRE<S-SIN>GS	24.	R/ASH
9.	EATEN (Eton)	25.	RISING
10.	EG/REGIO(n)/US	26.	SAINT JOHN (anag)
11.	ENNEAGON (anag)	27.	SINISTRA/L (anag)
12.	ETNA (rev)	28.	S<NOW>-S/HOE
13.	F<INLAND>I/A	29.	STICK/ WITH
14.	G/RE-ENGAGE	30.	TRAC<K/ER> DOG
15.	(S)IBERIA	31.	TWENTY-ONE (vingt-et-un)
16.	IN<FERN>AL	32.	UNIONIST

Jigsaw No. 15 – APHORISTICAL

P	I	E	B	A	L	D		A	U	R	E	A	T	E
	N		E		A		A		N		V		E	
O	V	E	R	F	U	L	L		G	O	I	T	R	E
	O		N		G		U		U		T		R	
K	I	T	S	C	H		M	E	M	S	A	H	I	B
	C		T		A		N						E	
D	E	C	E	M	B	R	I	S	T		C	A	R	R
			I		L				H		O			
F	L	A	N		Y	E	S	T	E	R	M	O	R	N
	I				A				R		B		O	
P	A	S	S	W	O	R	D		M	O	U	S	S	E
	I		H		L		I		I		S		T	
A	S	C	E	N	D		S	E	D	I	T	I	O	N
	O		B		I		M		O		E		V	
A	N	T	A	R	E	S		P	R	I	D	I	A	N

1.	A/LUM/NI
2.	ANT/ARES
3.	A/SCEN(e)/D
4.	(l)AUREATE
5.	BERNSTEIN (anag)
6.	CARR(y on)
7.	COMB/ (b)USTED
8.	DECEMBRIST (anag)
9.	E/VITA
10.	FLAN (hidden)
11.	GO/IT/RE
12.	IN/VOICE
13.	KIT<SC>H
14.	LA/UG<HAB(it)>LY
15.	LI<A/IS>ON
16.	MEM-<SAH/I>B(ers)
17.	MOUS<S>E
18.	OL/DIE
19.	OVERFULL (anag)
20.	PAS/SWORD
21.	PIE/BALD (uncovered)
22.	PR/IDIAN
23.	ROST/OVA
24.	SAD/IS/M
25.	S/EDITION
26.	SHE/BA
27.	T<ERR>IER
28.	THERMIDOR
29.	UNG/UM
30.	YES/TERM/OR/N

Jigsaw No. 16 – APHORISTICAL

M	O	P	E	D		O	E	N	O	T	H	E	R	A
Y		R		A		N		I		H		X		V
T	E	E	S	H	O	T		S	Q	U	E	E	Z	E
H		M		L		H		S		M		C		R
I	R	I	S		H	E	R	E	A	B	O	U	T	S
C		E		V		L		N		S		T		E
A	I	R	L	I	N	E	S		I	C	I	E	R	
L			C		E		S		R				R
	K	E	A	T	S		T	O	W	E	R	S	E	Y
A		A		O		B		U		W		T		E
M	I	T	H	R	A	I	S	T	S		A	R	A	B
E		W		I		A		H		W		A		R
L	I	E	D	O	W	N		E	N	H	A	N	C	E
I		L		U		C		N		E		G		A
A	L	L	I	S	S	A	I	D		N	O	E	N	D

1. AIR/LINES
2. See 32
3. A/M/ELIA
4. ARAB
5. A/VERSE
6. BIANCA (anag)
7. DAHL(ia)
8. E/AT/ WELL
9. ENHANCE (anag)
10. EXE/CUTE
11. HEREABOUTS (anag)
12. I<CIE>R
13. IRIS(h)
14. KEATS (the 'aphorism' is the epitaph he wrote for himself)
15. LIE D/OWN
16. MIT<HRAIS>TS

17. MOPED
18. MY/THIC(k)/A/L
19. NIS/SEN
20. NO END
21. OEN/OTHER/A
22. ON TH/E. LEE
23. PREMIER
24. RYE/ BREAD
25. SOU<THE>ND
26. SQUEEZE
27. ST/RANGE
28. TEE S/HOT
29. THUMBS/CREW
30. TOW/(j)ERSEY
31. VIC<TOR>IOUS
32,2. WHEN ALL IS SAID (and done) (anag)

139

Jigsaw No. 17 – APHORISTICAL

1. A/BIG/'AIL
2. ABO/UK/IR
3. ADONAI'S
4. AD/RIA/NA (all rev)
5. AENEAS (hidden)
6. (m)AGNATE
7. ALL/EG<R>O
8. ANNU(s)/LAR
9. A/SCRIBE
10. A/W<A/IT>ED
11. BANDI/COOT
12. BARRI<CAD>E
13. BE<ANFE>AST
14. CORIN(th)
15. DABBLE
16. DRE<AM>Y

17. DUCKS
18. FASTNESS
19. HART/N/ELL
20. IONIC (hidden)
21. KIT'S/CH
22. LOG/ EFFECT
23. MAN/'TIS
24. NE<AR B>Y
25. NOVELLAS (anag)
26. SALE/RN/O
27. SÈVRES (rev)
28. SPAS/M
29. SUBS/OIL
30. T<HANK>EE
31. VIL<LAG>E
32. WAR/D M/AID

Jigsaw No. 18 – APHORISTICAL

F	L	A	G	O	N	S		E	A	S	T	E	R	N
	O		R		O		K		G		H		O	
I	R	R	A	D	I	A	N	C	E		O	P	A	L
	C		V		S		I		I		U		D	
W	A	T	E	R	I	N	G		S	E	S	A	M	E
	S		E		H			T			E			
O	H	D	E	A	R		T	I	S	H	B	I	T	E
	O		N			S				E		A		
G	L	A	D	S	O	M	E		A	W	H	I	L	E
	L			S		R		G		E				
C	Y	P	R	U	S		R	E	A	R	M	I	C	E
	T		A		I		A		M		O		E	
A	R	T	Y		C	O	N	J	E	C	T	U	R	E
	E		O		L		T		T		H		N	
L	E	A	N	D	E	R		F	E	A	S	T	E	D

1. AGA/METE
2. A<GEIST>S
3. ARTY
4. AWHILE (anag)
5. BE<HE/MO>THS
6. C/ERNE
7. CONJ<ECT>URE
8. CY<P>RUS
9. E/ASTERN
10. FEASTED (anag)
11. FLA<GO>NS
12. GLADSOME (anag)
13. GRAVE'S/END
14. HOL<LY TRE(anag)>E
15. IRRADIANCE (anag)
16. K<NIGHTS/-ER/R>ANT
17. LEA<N>DER
18. LORCA (hidden)
19. NOISIER (anag)
20. O<H> DE/AR
21. O/PAL
22. OSSICLE (anag)
23. RAY/ON
24. REARM/ICE
25. ROAD-METAL (anag)
26. SE/SAME
27. THOUS(and)
28. TI<SH/BIT>E
29. WATERING

Jigsaw No. 19 – APHORISTICAL

THERE SHALL BE NO MORE LAND, SAY FISH (R.Brooke)

1. AIR-/MISS	17. IT/CH
2. AMA<RANT>H	18. JANEITE (jay night)
3. A/RAN	19. KILN/ER
4. A/TROP/IN (Belladonna)	20. MERRY MAY (Merimée)
5. BAN/QUETS	21. MYTHISM (hidden)
6. C<A/J>OLE	22. NIR<VAN>A
7. CH<ARAB>ANC(e)	23. PARLEYVOOS (anag)
8. C(d)OLLY BIRDS	24. PSYCHOSIS (anag)
(12 days of Chr)	25. RE<LIE>VE
9. COME UP	26. RHEO/TOMES
10. CONSTABLE	27. RHIZOME (rise 'ome)
11. CRIES	28. SEED CASE (anag)
12. EUROPA	29. SPENS(er)
13. FRET	30. SUPPLY LINE
14. HA<R>TS	31. SWEDE
15. HENRY MOORE (anag)	32. TYPE
16. (l)IBERIAN	

142

Jigsaw No. 20 – APHORISTICAL

Shaded squares: THAT WHICH HATH MADE THEM DRUNK HATH MADE ME BOLD (*Macbeth* **II.2.1**)

1. ARRIERE (pensée)
2. AT/ THE RE/ADY
3. BODYWORK
4. B<R>EAST
5. BROU(brew)/HAHA
6. CADE/AUX
7. CUT/ CORNER/S(hop)
8. DI<SUN/IT>Y
9. DO/OR
10. (H)ENRI/CH
11. FRES(rev)/H AIR
12. FUEL (anag)
13. GO/L<I>ATH
14. HARE/'LD
15. HE<B>R/E-W
16. I/AM/BIC <'VE>RSE
17. M<ERR/I>E
18. N/OR/M
19. O/D<D/ F>ISH
20. ODES/SA
21. PARIS/H
22. SMASHING
23. STAY
24. STRA(rev)/W HAT
25. ST/RIFE
26. TACKY
27. T(s)ENSIBLE
28. YE/OMAN/RY

Jigsaw No. 21 – APHORISTICAL

Shaded squares: NOTHING/ SHOULD E<VE>R/ BE D/ONE/ FOR TH/E/ FIRS/T T/I/ME

1. A/BA/TABLE
2. AG/E(cstasy)
3. BOOTS/TRAP
4. CO<ST/L>Y
5. DEEP WATER (weep daughter)
6. EEL(rev)
7. EPEE (hidden)
8. EPHRAIM (anag)
9. F/L/A/B
10. FLOYD (anag)
11. FR/EES/TONE
12. GO/T ON
13. LA/DY ANNA (anag)
14. LO/PER
15. LUM/ME
16. MOORE
17. NORI(rev)/EGA (rev)
18. OBSER(anag)/VER (rev)
19. ONE-NOUGHT (1/0)
20. O/VERT
21. PIANO/FORTE
22. PLA<I>CE
23. PRO/PANE
24. RE/TYPE
25. S/ASHES
26. SEE T(rev)/O
27. STAR TABLES
28. TOL<D A TA>L/E
29. T<RASH/ C>AN
30. TUT/OR
31. TWO A PENNY (anag)
    (Hot cross buns – nursery rhyme)

144

Jigsaw No. 22 – APHORISTICAL

S	H	O				E	I		N
W	E	E	P	I	E	S		S	H	A	W	N	E	E
I	M		L		E		T		T	G	A
T	O	P	A	S		L	A	U	N	D	E	R	E	R
C			I	F		B		I		A	E
H	I	G	H	L	O	W		G	R	E	T	N	A
	H		K		I		G		T		I	S
G	R	O	T		S	L	E	E	P		W	A	I	T
U		S		D		L		O	G		T
I	A	T	R	I	C		D	R	A	W	E	R	S
L		T		G	D	E		N			Y
D	A	R	K	R	O	O	M	S		D	R	E	G	S
E		A		E		M		I		A	G	T
R	E	I	S	S	U	E		C	O	L	O	G	N	E
S		N		S				F		S	M

1.	COLOGNE	16.	HIGH-LOW
	(Eau de; Coleridge poem)	17.	I/'AT/RIC(k)
2.	DARK/ROOMS	18.	INGRATIATE (in grey she ate)
3.	DIG/RE/SS	19.	LA/UNDER/ER
4.	DO/ME	20.	NE<AR EA>ST
5.	DRAWERS	21.	OIL/-SILK
6.	DR<EG>S	22.	REISSUE (hidden)
7.	EAT DIRT (anag)	23.	S<ELF>-WILL
8.	E<GG>S	24.	SHAW/NEE
9.	(kin)G/AND/ALF	25.	SLEEP (rev)
10.	GEODESIC (hidden)	26.	STUB (rev)
11.	G<HOST> TRAIN	27.	SWITCH
12.	GRE/TNA (all rev)	28.	SY/STEM
13.	GROT	29.	TOP/AS (Twelfth Night)
	(T.E. Browne poem)	30.	W/AIT
14.	GUILD-ERS	31.	WEE/PIES
15.	HEMP		

Jigsaw No. 23 – APHORISTICAL

Shaded squares: MISS/IS/S(l)IP/PI/ MUD <P>IE; DEATH BY CHOCOLATE (anag)

1. ABS/TA/IN	16. ME<NI>AL
2. (b)ABY/SMAL(l)	17. O/CC/ULT
3. ADDENDA (anag)	18. ONSET (anag)
4. A/LAME/IN	19. RE/C/HATE
5. A/P<PL/A(rev)>UD	20. RIDGE
6. APPR<A>ISE	21. SC<HIED>AM
7. BA/BY/HOOD	22. SISLEY (sizzly)
8. BAMBOO(z/led)	23. SPECTRAL (anag)
9. BASS/I/NETS	24. STAKE
10. BRA<SS>Y	25. STEEPS
11. BULKINESS (anag)	26. TA<NAI(anag)>STES
12. (s)ENTRY	27. T/HEIST
13. LOOSEN (anag)	28. TWIT/CH
14. MADDEN (hidden)	29. UN/BO(u)LTING
15. MALL/ECHO	30. UNSIGNED (anag)

Jigsaw No. 24 – APHORISTICAL

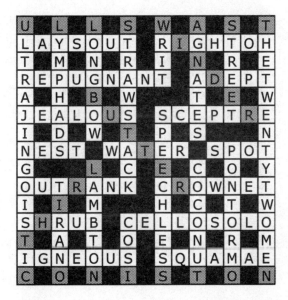

Shaded squares are British Lakes: ULLS, WAST and CONISTON (water), and WINDER, BUTTER and THIRL (mere).

1. A/DEPT	16. RE<PU>GNANT
2. AG<NAT>ES	17. RIG/H/T-O/H
3. CELL<O>SOLO	18. SCEPT(ical)/RE
4. COCO/NUT	19. SH/RUB
5. COS/I	20. SPEECHLESS (anag)
6. CROW/NET	21. SPOT
7. IGNEOUS (anag)	22. S/QUA/MAE
8. J{E}ALOUS{e}	23. STRAW' S/TACK
9. LAMB/TON	24. S<TREE>T
10. LAYS OUT	25. THE/ TWENTY/-T/WO MEN
11. LONG/BOW	26. TIR<AN>O
12. LYMPH/ADS	27. ULTRA-JINGOISTIC (anag)
13. (ho)NEST	28. WATER
14. O<UTRAN(anag)>K	29. WRIT
15. PONT/OR/MO	

Jigsaw No. 25 – APHORISTICAL

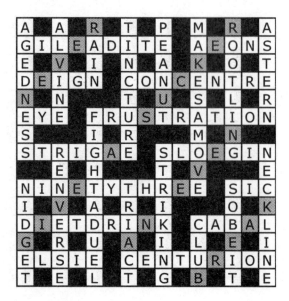

Shaded squares: NEVER GIVE A SUCKER AN EVEN BREAK (Groucho Marx)

1.	AEONS (anag)	16.	MA<K>E/S A MOV(ar)/E
2.	A<GE/DNES(rev)>S	17.	NECK/LINE
3.	AL<VIN>E	18.	NID/GET
4.	ASTER/N	19.	NINETY-THREE (anag)
5.	CABAL(lero)	20.	PEANUT
6.	CE/N/TURI<O>N	21.	RAIN (reign)
7.	CLUB	22.	RENVERSE (anag)
8.	CONCENTR(at)E	23.	R[O]OT/LING[o]
9.	DEIGN (Dane)	24.	SIC(k)
10.	DIET/-DR/INK	25.	SLOE/ GIN
11.	ELS<I>E	26.	SOB/EIT
12.	EYE	27.	STRIGAE (anag)
13.	F<IGH/T A D>UEL	28.	STRIKING
14.	F<RUST/RAT>I/ON	29.	TIN/CTURE
15.	G<I/LEAD>ITE	30.	TR<I>ACT

Jigsaw No. 26 – DIAMETRICAL

Diameters: GOOSEBERRY-/STONE and RASPBERRY/ RIPPLE

1. AB/SORBS
2. BROW<N>SE/A
3. CAREER
4. C<'ORRID>OR
5. DESTROYERS (anag)
6. DO<W>SE
7. EASES (hidden)
8. ELAPSE (anag)
9. ELL/A
10. ESSENE (E,S,N)
11. FAT-<FRE>E
12. FITTER
13. GLAD/BACH
14. HEARTS ARE TRUMPS
15. LORD/ ALIVE
16. MA/INROAD
17. O HELL (hello)
18. OR/DINE/E
19. REP/UGN
20. S<ALAN/G>ANE
21. SEA/REDNESS (Macb 2.2.59)
22. SHE/A/-TREE
23. STRUT
24. S<YEN>ITE
25. TAR-B<R>USH
26. THE PRINCE (anag)
27. TRE<SS>Y
28. VI/EW
29. WATER PUMP (anag)

Jigsaw No. 27 – DIAMETRICAL

Diagonals: DOCTOR'S DISCIPLE (Shaw: D's dilemma, Devil's d.); TI<TU{S ANDRO}NIC>US (suit, rev).

1. (p)ASCOLI
2. ASTRICT (anag)
3. AUTU(m)N
4. BI<GOT>S
5. BLE/RIOT
6. CHAS/M
7. CO<UR/TED DA(anag)>NGER
8. DEIRDRE (anag)
9. DO-G/O/ODER
10. (uei)DRAPED (hidden rev)
11. EAT TRIPE
12. GRAIN
13. HIGH CHAIR
14. I/AM/B<IS>T
15. INDIAN ROPE (anag)
16. INNER (shooting)
17. IN/SPAN (1 + 9 inches)
18. LYALL (hidden)
19. MO/HO
20. MURCHISON
21. NOT/CHELS(ea)
22. (crypt)OGAM
23. OVER/ACTS
24. PHO/TOGRAM (rev)
25. ROSS/O
26. T<HAR D>ESERT
27. TIN/GLE
28. TREN<E>T
29. TUTORSHIP (anag)

Jigsaw No. 28 – RHOMBICAL

L	O	S	T	W	O	R	L	D		B	A	S	I	S
Y		I		H		E		E		U		E		T
R	E	D	H	I	L	L		B	A	R	O	Q	U	E
I		O		T		A		U		R		U		V
C	O	N	T	E	S	T	A	N	T		N	O	S	E
		I		W		E		K		B		I		N
F	L	E	S	H	E	D		S	U	L	T	A	N	A
A			A						A					G
I	D	Y	L	L	I	C		L	U	C	E	R	N	E
R		A		E		O		I		K		I		
F	E	R	N		B	R	I	T	I	S	H	L	A	W
I		D		G		N		H		T		I		R
G	A	L	I	L	E	E		I	S	O	G	E	N	Y
H		E		U		R		U		N		V		E
T	H	Y	M	E		S	O	M	M	E	L	I	E	R

Rhombus: A LITTLE LEARNING : A DANGEROUS THING

1. BAR<O>QUE
2. BAS<I>S
3. BLACK/STONE
4. BRITISH LAW (anag)
5. BURR
6. CONTE<STA>NT
7. CORN/ER'S
8. DE/BUNKS
9. FAIR/ FIG/HT
10. (In)FERN(o)
11. FLE/SHED
12. G<ALI>LEE
13. G/L/U/E
14. IDYLLIC (anag) (LYCID/I/L)
15. IS/OGE/NY
16. LIT/HI<U>M

17. LOST WORLD
18. LUCERNE
19. LYRIC (hidden)
20. NOSE (knows)
21. RED/HILL
22. RELATED (anag)
23. RI/LIE/VI
24. SE<QUOI(t)>A
25. SIDON/IE
26. (con)SOMME/LIE/R
27. ST<EVEN>AGE
28. SULTANA
29. THYME (time)
30. WHIT/E W<HAL>E
31. W<RYE>R
32. YARD/LEY

Jigsaw No. 29 – RHOMBICAL

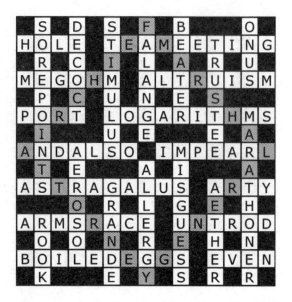

Rhombus: AIR-CHIEF-MARSHAL and ATTORNEY-GENERAL (anag)

1. A/EROS/OL
2. A/ETHER
3. ALL/ERGY (anag)
4. AL/TRUISM
5. (s)AND AL/SO
6. ARMS/ RACE
7. (he)ARTY
8. ASTRAGALUS
9. BEATER
10. BO<I/LED/ EG>GS
    (soldiers = bread & butter)
11. DEC/OCT
12. EVEN
13. F/A/L/A/N/G/E
14. GRANDE
15. See 22

16. IMP/EARL
17. LOGARITHMS (anag) (glamor)
18. MARAT/HON/ER
19. ME<GOH(rev)>M(sahib)
20. MIS<GUES(t)>S
21. O/NUS(rev)
22,15. PORT/HOLE
23. ROOK
24. SORE POINTS (anag)
25. STI<MUL>US (all rev)
26. TEA-M/EETING
27. TRU<STE>E
28. UNTROD (anag)
    (Wordsworth: 'She dwelt among
    the untrodden ways')

152

Jigsaw No. 30 – RHOMBICAL

Rhombus: EVERLASTING LIFE and ETERNAL TRIANGLE

1. A/CAR/I
2. A/GAIN
3. AG<ON/IS>E
4. AIRSHAFT (anag)
5. ALMANAC (hidden)
6. AND/ROME/DA
7. BA/SIC
8. BUFF/ALOES
9. CH<ELON>IAN
10. D/WELT
11. EL/TO/N
12. (p)ENDLE/SS
13. EOSIN (hidden)
14. FLO<RE>AT
15. F<RAT>RY
16. HIERATIC (higher attic) (priestly)
17. IMP/A/LA
18. INERTIA
19. (beg)INNER
20. NOTORIETY (anag)
21. (ap)OSTLE/R
22. OTHER/WISE
23. O/VER IT(y)
24. PENT/ACLE
25. READ/MIT
26. (f)RIDGE
27. SE<MIN>ATED
28. S<POND>EE
29. STRANGER
30. TEARSHEET (anag)
31. TI<T/MIC>E
32. TYR<ANNO>US (Tyrus, Latin for Tyre)

153

Jigsaw No. 31 – RHOMBICAL

Rhombus: GOD REST YOU MERRY GENTS IT'S XMAS DAY

1. ACTS UP (catsup)
2. A/M<P>UTE/E
3. ANNUL/US
4. APSE (anag)
5. A/ST/RIDE
6. BLANQUETTE (blanket)
7. CAN'T/A/TRICE
8. COL/IT/IS
9. CR/A/XI (all rev)
10. CUR/MUD/GEON
11. END/EAR
12. FORM <MAST>ER
13. GLARE (anag)
14. GRACE/ CUP
15. HU<MORI'S>T
16. I/DI-OTIC
17. JE/A/LOUSY
18. JUMBLE
19. L/AIR
20. MATISSE (anag)
21. (So/lo)MON/GOLIA(th)
22. OENOPHIL (anag)
23. OPEN/-PLAN
24. O/USE
25. PA'S/TRY
26. PUL<TEN>E/Y
27. PUR/CELL
28. REA<L>M
29. SIGN
30. SILENCER
31. SPEC/TRA
32. S/TEAL

154

Jigsaw No. 32 – RHOMBICAL

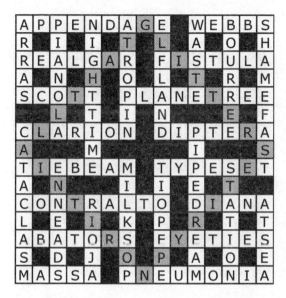

Rhombus: ALL THAT GLITTERS/ AIN'<T IRO>N PY(anag)/RITES

1. ABAT(t)O(i)RS
2. A<P/PEN>DAGE
3. ARRAS (hidden)
4. AT<R>/OP/IN
5. AT SEA
6. BOUR<RE(s)>E
7. CAT/A/CLA<S>M
8. CLA<RIO>N
9. CONTRALTO (anag)
10. (in)DIANA
11. DIP/T/ERA
12. EL<FLAN>D
13. ENNE(any)/ADS
14. EYE/TIES
15. FIST/'ULA
16. MASS/A
17. M<ILKS>OP
18. NIGH/T-T/I/ME
    (S. Holmes story)
19. PIANOLA (anag)
20. PI<P>E D/REAM
21. PLANE T/RE/E
22. PNEUMON(new mown)/I/A
23. REAL/GAR(rev)
24. RI<OJ>A (all rev)
25. SCOTT
26. SHAM/EFAST (anag)
27. S<TATI>ON
28. TIE/ BEAM
29. TIO PEPE
30. TYPE<SE>T (anag)
31. WASTE (waist)
32. WEBBS (lettuce)

Jigsaw No. 33 – PERIMETRICAL

Perimeter: SPEAK SOFTLY AND CARRY A BIG STICK (anag) (Theodore Roosevelt) (in *Oxford Dictionary of Quotations*)

1. A/E/ROBES
2. ALL A(h)/T SEA
3. A/P/LOMB(ardy)
4. CAPABILITY
5. CARP/ET-MOTH
6. C<LEAN TO>WEL
7. CON/TOUR
8. DAT<UR>A
9. DORA (defence of the realm act)
10. EAST (hidden)
11. GEAR
12. GLUT(inous)
13. HARM/ONIC
14. IMBER/T
15. IN HALF (inhale)
16. INKY (pinky parleyvoo)
17. K/A/MIK<A/Z>E
18. KIT/H AND/ KIN
19. LI<TIG(er)/AT/I>ON
20. OLD AGE (anag)
21. P/IMPLY
22. SALLY/ BROWN *
23. SA<VAN>NAH
24. SHO<W/BOA>T
25. S<KETCH>Y
26. THE ALPS (hidden)
27. UNAF/RAID
28. W/HAT

* Faithless Sally Brown, poem by Hood (the one which ends 'they went and told the sexton and the sexton tolled the bell').

Jigsaw No. 34 – PERIMETRICAL

Perimeter: THESE <BOOT>S/ WE/RE MADE/ FOR <WAL>K/IN/G (Nancy Sinatra)

1. ALARM-RADIO (anag)
2. A/L<TAR> P/ARTY
3. AVER/RHO/IS/M
4. BALA(laika)
5. B/L<U>E VEL/VET
6. BOO/R
7. EAR-WIT/NESS
8. ERAS(e)
9. ETHE (hidden)
10. FEDERALISE (anag)
11. GO T/O MAR/KET
12. HO/OP
13. IMP/ACTIONS
14. KNEADED
15. LIAR (rev)
16. L/IN/O
17. L/YAM
18. NEAP(olitan)
19. ON/US
20. PUFF
21. P<UR/VI>EW
22. SK(y)/ELTON
23. SQUARE/ YARD
24. SUPERSTORE (anag)
25. T<OK>EN/-MON/EY
26. UPGRADE (anag)
27. W<AD>I
28. WILDEBEEST(gnu, noo)

157

Jigsaw No. 35 – PERIMETRICAL

Perimeter: LONDON AND NORTH-EASTERN RAILWAY

1. A/LASS/I/O
2. A/LIE/NATION
3. AN<T-B/IR>DS
4. A/TT/LEE
5. AU/TO/MOBILE
6. D<OG/-S>HOW
7. ERIE (eerie)
8. INSPECTION COVER (anag)
9. LAWN
10. L<INK/AG>E
11. NECROLOGIC (anag)
12. N/ERNST
13. NICE

14. OFF-BREAK
15. OIL-PAINT (anag)
16. ON THE RUN (anag)
17. OT/IS
18. P/ALL/OR
19. ROB/OTI<C>S
20. S<LOV>AKI/A
21. ST/ITCH
22. SUN-G/OD (rev)
23. TA<LENT>LE/SS
24. TIT/'OIST
25. WATERLOO/ STATION
26. YAF/FLE (rev)

Jigsaw No. 36 – PERIMETRICAL

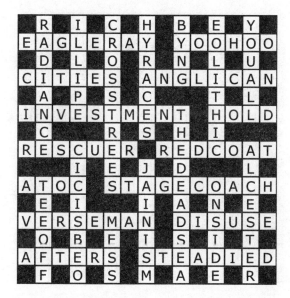

Perimeter: RICH BEYOND THE DREAMS OF AVARICE

1. AFTER/S
2. ALCESTER (anag)
3. AN<G/L/IC>AN
4. ATOC (anag)
5. BYNG (Voltaire)
6. CIC/IS/BE/O
7. CI/TIES
8. CROSS/TREES
9. D/ISUSE (anag)
10. E/AGLE-<RA>Y
11. E<O/LI>THIC
12. HOLD
13. HY/RACES
14. ILL/IPE
15. INVESTMENT
16. JA<IN/IS>M
17. MESS
18. ONSIDE
19. RA<DIAN>CE
20. REDCOAT (anag)
21. RESCUER
22. STAGE/COACH
23. STE<AD/I>ED
24. TEE OFF (anag)
25. THE DEAD/ SEA(ts)
26. VER/SE-MAN (rev)
27. YOO-HOO (you who)
28. YOU-ALL

159

Jigsaw No. 37 – PERIMETRICAL

Perimeter: YOU HAVE DELIGHTED US LONG ENOUGH
(*Pride and Prejudice*)

1. AFTERS/HAVE
2. ANI<MA>LS
3. BACK/GROUND
4. BUHL (boule)
5. CHURCH <RO>(I)LL
6. CON/VERGING
7. E<GG/L>'ER
8. ENCEPHALON (anag)
9. ENTRÉE
10. FRI/END
11. GOO/GOL
12. (ma)G<RAN/IT>IC
13. HE<A/CH/A>M
14. HE/BRAISE
15. LENINIST (anag)
16. LO/GO
17. MONMOUTH
    (Henry V & Duke 1685)
18. NICE
19. NON-U(plet)
20. ODO/ROUS
21. ORANGE TREE (anag)
22. P/ADDING/TO/N
23. PAS/COLI
24. (Coma)TO/SE(a)
25. UIST (hidden)
26. UPPER/ CLASS
27. VIET (vi et armis)
28. YEA/R

Jigsaw No. 38 – PERIMETRICAL

Perimeter: HAL/F A L/OAF/ IS BETTER THAN/ NO B/READ

1. ABER/RATION
2. A/PERI/ENT
3. AR<GEN>T
4. ARTEMIS (anag)
5. ASKE(y)
6. ATTENDANCE
7. BROADS/WORD
8. CHIEF RABBI(t) (Watership Down)
9. DEER-HAIR (anag)
10. EAST (anag)
11. FAR/E <DO>DGER
12. FRANC/IS
13. HEAT
14. LAO<DICEAN>S
15. LE<STRAD>E
16. L<I/M>B
17. LOT/TIE
18. NO/SING
19. OP<PRO/BR>IUM
20. OTTO
21. RED STAR
22. SHERPA (anag)
23. SIGH (hidden)
24. SLAVONIA
25. SO/LID-STATE (anag)
26. T<I>NT
27. TURF
28. WO<O>LF/AT

Jigsaw No. 39 – PERIMETRICAL

Perimeter: M/OZ/ART: S/YM/PHONY/ NO. THIRTY-SIX IN C (anag) (known as 'The Linz')

1. ANALYST (annalist)
2. AS<QUIT>H
3. B<ANN>ERET
4. CALM/ DOWN
5. ENSIGN/SHIP
6. FINO (hidden)
7. FOR<SY>TH
8. GESUNDHEIT (anag)
9. HAR/MAN
10. IN/ A WAY
11. INDIAN CORN (anag)
12. INF/O
13. LIEGEDOM (anag)
14. MAROON
15. NA/A/MAN
16. NIS/I (rev)
17. NOUNAL (anag naunal)
18. OLD WINDSOR
19. (w)O/MEN
20. RE/DO
21. RIDE
22. SAX/ONIST
23. SEE<D>INGS (anag)
24. TAKES SNUFF (anag)
25. THIRD DAY (anag)
26. X/BODIES
27. YE <GOD>S
28. ZOLLVER(solver)/EIN

Jigsaw No. 40 – PERIMETRICAL

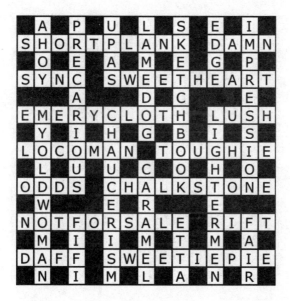

Perimeter: A PULSE IN THE ETERNAL MIND, NO LESS
(cf sonnet, 'If I should die …')

1. A/HOY
2. CA<RA>MEL
3. CHALKSTONE (anag)
4. CH<AUC/E>RISM
5. DAFF
6. DAM/N
7. EDGE
8. EMERY/-CLOTH
9. ET/TA (Etta Place, K. Ross's part)
10. FAIR
11. F/I/F/I
12. I'M/PRESS<I>ON
13. LA<ME DO(c)>G
14. LI<GH/TERM>EN

15. LOCO/MAN
16. LUSH
17. MY OLD WOMAN (anag)
18. N/OT FOR SALE (anag)
19. ODDS
20. PREC<A/R>IOUS
21. RIFT
22. SHORT/ PLANK
23. S/K<ETC/H-B>OOK
24. SYNC (sink)
25. SW<E.E./T-HE>ART
26. SWEETIE/-PIE
27. TO<UGH/I>E
28. UPAS (hidden)

163

Jigsaw No. 41 – PERIMETRICAL

Perimeter: CANNOT BE NAMED FOR LEGAL REASONS (anag)

1. AMP/HORAE
2. A/NAG/RAM
3. ANON
4. BLUEBREAST (anag)
5. C<L>UE
6. C/RIPPLE
7. DEREGULATE (anag)
8. EME<RY/PAP>ER
9. FO<IBL>E
10. FO/RA
11. GALL/OP/ER
12. HALF-A-DOZE/N
13. IN/FO
14. LEAVE/ OFF
15. M<ANAG>ERIAL
16. N/AR<N>IA
17. NESH (hidden)
18. NEW/-LAID (all rev)
19. NIGHT-BLIND
20. OFF/A
21. OPP<R>O/BR<I>UM
22. O/VID
23. PAN/G
24. POLY/NO/MIAL (meal)
25. RA/TION
26. S<LEEK>IT
27. SLIM LINE (anag)
28. TIP-/OFF

Jigsaw No. 42 – PERIMETRICAL

Perimeter: A/BAND/ON/ ALL HOPE/ YE W/HO E/NTER HERE (anag)

1. AI/R IND/IA
2. ANA/GRAMS
3. A/THEN/S
4. BEAT/RICE
5. CO<ME>DY
6. DIVINE
7. DRY/DEN
8. DU/MP
9. ELEVEN PLUS
10. ELSPETH (anag)
11. ESTIMATION (anag)
12. ETNEAN (anag)
13. FOOL
14. GRAND HOTEL (anag)
15. H/ELLIS/H
16. HOW ELSE (Howells)
17. LATE SHOW (anag)
18. NAV(rev)/ARIN (anag)
19. NINE-FOOT (anag)
20. ONE-OFF
21. ON/SIDE
22. O/VERLAIN(e)
23. PARAD<IS>E
24. PU<E>R(ga)TO RI<C>O
25. PUNCTO (anag)
26. REED (deer)
27. REST
28. TINNITUS

Jigsaw No. 43 – PERIMETRICAL

Perimeter: IT IS NO USE CRYING / OVER SPIL<T MI>L/K

1. ASS/IS/I	15. KNO<W/AB>LE
2. A/TAP	16. LABOURED (anag)
3. A/Z/O/V	17. LACE/RATE(anag)
4. CAS(s)INO	18. LEMNOS (anag)
5. C/IN/NAM/O/NI/C	19. MI<SCA>LL
6. COLE/ PORTER	20. NONCHALAN(anag)/T
7. COLY	21. OCHREOUS (anag)
8. COMPO/RTS	22. OR/CH/IS
9. CROW/N INN(y)	23. SE<A-LAN>E
10. IAN/THE	24. TAP<ST>ER
11. I/B/IS	25. TEAM SPIRIT (anag)
12. I/DEAL/I/SING	26. TR<AD>UCE
13. INTERSTICE (anag)	27. TWIN/GE
14. ISLE (hidden)	28. U(w)IST

Jigsaw No. 44 – PERIMETRICAL

Perimeter: REVENGE IS A DISH BEST SERVED COLD (anag)

1.   A/DON/AI
2.   AN/CE/STRESS
3.   B<O'LD>EST
4.   CANINE
5,13. COS/I (n)FAN T/UTTE(r)
6.   CRO<F>TER
7.   DAM/NATIONS
     (Browning, Spanish cloister)
8.   DEN/ARIUS
9.   E<ARNE>D
10. EARWITNESS (anag)
11. ECRU (hidden)
12. ESTUARY
13. See 5
14. G<O>IN/G OUT
15. L/ORD <ARCH>ER
16. LOUNGE SUIT (anag)
17. MARS
18. MODERNNESS (anag)
19. NAST
20. N/E/W/S
21. OL<I>D
22. RE/NO
23. S<CAT>HED
24. STAB
25. S<US/ANNA>H
26. TERRAC(e)/OTT/A
27. VECTOR (anag)
28. VINE/ STREET

167

Jigsaw No. 45 – PERIMETRICAL

Perimeter: I ENDEAVOUR TO GIVE SATISFACTION

1. AG<ES P>(h)AST (hymn)
2. (Pyth)AGORAS
3. ANGUIS(h)
4. ARP/EGG/IO
5. BOR/ZO/I (all rev)
6. CANNON-SHOT (billiards)
7. CAR<D> P/LAYER
8. CASS<I/OPE>IA
9. CON/TEST
10. DA<STAR>D
11. ENSIGN
12. EPANAPHORA (anag)
13. FILM-GOER (anag)
14. I AM SORRY (anag)

15. I/RAN
16. NAG/A
17. NAR<NI>A (rev)
18. NASSAU (hidden)
19. O/SC<IT>ANT
20. PAPER/ BAG
21. PAST/RAM/I
22. PU<B>S
23. SAKHAR(anag)/OV(a)
24. S/ART/RE(veals)
25. SE/KO
26. TEMP/ERA
27. TYM<P>ANO (anag)
28. VI<VAC>E

168

Jigsaw No. 46 – PERIMETRICAL

Perimeter: I/ CAME L/I/KE W/ATER AND L(anag)/I/KE W/IND I GO

1. A{E<ROME>TRI}C
2. AIR/LIE
3. AR<CAD>IA
4. BEIN(g)
5. C/ART<O/ON>IST
6. CIRL (Searle)
7. CREW
8. C<RIB/BAG>E
9. DEANERY (anag)
10. DRY-/CELL
11. ELI/XIR (rev)
12. E<NCO>RE
13. ETNA (hidden)
14. GR/A/L-LOCH
15. I/CAR/US
16. I/NAP/PETE/NT
17. IN/FRINGE
18. INSIGNIA (anag)
19. IN THE (d)ARK
20. IR/VINE
21. LEPRECHAUN (anag)
22. MI<CHA>EL
23. NESH (hidden)
24. ON<SID>E
25. PUNCH-/DRUNK
26. SUFI (suffit)
27. T<ERROR>ISED
28. WRON/GFUL (anags)

169

Jigsaw No. 47 – PERIMETRICAL

Perimeter: THE GIRL I SAW YOU WITH AT BRIGHTON

1. ANGLES/EY (rev)
2. DECREE NISI
3. ETC/H
4. E<U/DO>RA
5. E<XI>T
6. G/HILL/IE
7. GOO/D AT
8. HELO/DEA (hallo dear)
9. HELVETII (anag)
10. HOL/OF/ERNES
11. HOT AND COLD
12. IDLE FELLOW (anag) (Jerome K J, book)
13. I'LL/-FEE/LING
14. JIM(gymn)/CROW
15. LI/NEAR
16. NASO (hidden & lit.)
17. NASSAU (anag)
18. NO/T OUT (cricket)
19. ODD/ JOB
20. OLGA (anag)
21. OPEN/SHAW (S. Holmes story)
22. OVER T/HE S/E/A
23. REAR
24. RO<PINE>SS
25. TALLIS/H
26. TAN/DOOR/I
27. TOLL-GATE (goal Tate)
28. WONT

Jigsaw No. 48 – PERIMETRICAL

Perimeter and 14: FOUR AND TWENTY BLACKBIRDS BAKED IN A PIE (…began to sing: O wasn't that a dainty dish to set before the king).

1. A/BET
2. ANTARCTICA (anag)
3. A/PI/ARIST(o)
4. ARGY/RITE
5. ARI<O>STO
6. BALSA/M
7. CAB/-RANK
8. DE<MON/IS>E
9. DOG-FANCIER (anag)
10. DOWN
11. EGGS
12. FOG/GI/A
13. HEAT/HEN
14. See perimeter

15. IPECAC (anag)
16. KALA(hari)/MDAN
17. MONDAY CLUB (anag)
18. NAIL
19. OF/F SEA(anag)/SONS
20. P<ALE/ YELL>OW
21. RAN/I
22. REACH FOR (anag)
23. RIFLING
24. S<HARD-BORN>E
25. SINFUL (hidden)
26. T<IM/E-B(rev)>OMB
27. TONY
28. U/NIP/ED

171

Jigsaw No. 49 – PERIMETRICAL

Perimeter: THE BOSOM OF HIS FATHER AND HIS GOD (anag) (Gray's Elegy)

1. ASTI (hidden)
2. A/T/TEST
3. BA<BY/-S>IT
4. BRA<INST/OR>M
5. DID/O (Merchant of V. V 1 10)
6. DISTRAUGHT (anag)
7. E/BULL/(sc)IENCE
8. G<R>AY
9. (Mata) HARI(jan)
10. HO<ME>LY
11. I'D/I/OT-P(anag)/ROOF
12. IN/CASE/MEN/T,
    IN/CASEMENT
13. MANDARIN
14. NATO (hidden)
15. O/BO<E PLA(anag)>YER
16. ONER (rev)
17. O/RATIONS
18. PEAR (pair)
19. PROPER/TIES
20. REGORGE (anag)
21. (p)RIGGISH
22. SELF
23. S<MET>AN/A
24. ST<ONER>AG (ragstone)
25. THECLA (hidden) (Hairstreak)
26. THIRTEENTH (anag)
27. TI<MB>ER
28. TRAV(esty)/IATA

Jigsaw No. 50 – PERIMETRICAL (Variant)

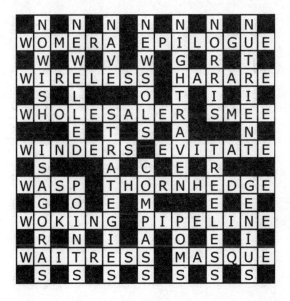

Perimeter: The 'rose' is a compass rose; the perimeter shows the compass points.

1,16. COMPASS/ POINTS	15. PI<PELI>NE
2. EPILOGUE (anag)	16. See 1
3. EVITA/TE	17. PO/MS
4. GENIUS (anag)	18. SMEE (anag)
5. H/A/RARE	19. ST<RAT/EG>IES
6. I<SAGO>RAS	20. THORN-<HE>DGE (anag)
7. MASQUE (hidden)	21. T<REEL>ESS
8. NAVE	22. WAITRESS (anag)
9. NE<WELL>ED	23. WAS/P
10. NEW S/'OLS	24. WHOLE/SALER (hole sailor)
11. NIGHT/-RAVEN (anag)	25. WINDERS
12. N/ORRIS	26. WI<RE>LES/S
13. NO/WISH	27. W<OK>ING
14. NUTRIENT (anag)	28. WOME(n)/RA

Jigsaw No. 51 – PERIMETRICAL

Perimeter: NO GO/OD D/E<ED EVER(deever)> GO/E/S
UN/PU<NI>SHED

1. BEN/EFAC(rev)/TOR
2. COME T/O LIFE (anag)
3. DEAD (hidden)
4. DIS/PRO/FESS
5. DOCKS WAGES (anag)
6. EAR/P
7. EUC(rev)/LID
8. GOLDEN GOAL (anag)
9. HA<N>S
10. I/M<AG>INE
11. INSTA<L/ME>NT
12. LOUNGE
13. NEURITIS (new rite is)
14. NIDULATION (anag)
15. NOEL/ COWARD
16. O'ERS/TED
17. O/GEE (O,G,S)
18. O/PAL
19. OS/LO
20. RUNNING DOG
21. SEASONS
22. SI/ME(mais)/NON
23. SPIV (vips, rev)
24. STEN/TORIAN (anag)
25. STOCK/(eg lemon-)ADE
26. TAB/U
27. UN/CO
28. URSA (hidden)

174

Jigsaw No. 52 – PERIMETRICAL

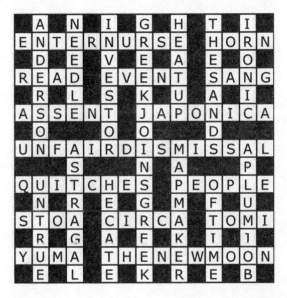

Perimeter: A NIGHT/IN/GALE (SANG) IN BERKELEY/ SQUARE

1. AND/'ER/SON	15. MA/P M/A/K/ER
2. A PLUM/ JOB	16. NEEDLE
3. AS/SENT	17. OF TIME (see 24)
4. ASTRA/GAL	18. PE<OP>LE
5. CIRCA(ssian)	19. QUI<T>CHES (c. grass)
6. ENTER NURSE (anag)	20. RE/AD
7. E/VENT	21. SANG (fr)
8. GREEK JOINS G(anag)/REEK	22. STOA (hidden)
9. HE<A>T UP	23. THE N/EW/ MOON
10. HE-CAT/E	24,17. THE SANDS OF TIME
11. HORN	25. TOM/I
12. IN/VEST/OR	26. UN-FAIR/ DI'S/MISSAL
13. IRON/I/C	27. 'UNT/RUE
14. JAPONICA (anag)	28. YUM/A

Jigsaw No. 53 – PERIMETRICAL

	I	T	S	T		O	P		P
N	A	Z	A	R	E	T	H		L	I	L	L	E	E
	I		C		N		E	D		E		N		
I	N	T	H	E	S	C	R	U	M		D	I	E	D
		Y		I		E		A		G		T		
A	F	R	O		B	R	O	W	N	B	E	A	R	S
	I		N		L		F					A		
G	L	O	S	T	E	R		H	A	W	O	R	T	H
	M				W		N		U		E		
A	S	T	O	N	I	S	H	E	D		T	O	D	O
	T		N		N		E		R		O		
O	U	C	H		G	A	N	G	O	F	F	O	U	R
	D		E		M		T		P		U		P
G	I	T	A	N	A		H	O	O	K	S	H	O	T
	O		T		R		E		V		E		N

Perimeter: IT STOPPED SHORT NEVER TO GO AGAIN (WHEN THE OLD MAN DIED)

1. A/FRO
2. AN/DROP/OV
3. ASTON/I/SHED
4. BROW/N B/EARS
5. DI<E>D
6. FILM STUDIO (anag)
7. GANG/ OF F/OUR
8. GITANA (hidden)
9. G/LOST/ER
10. HA/WORTH
11. HOOK/ SHOT
12. IA/IN
13. (k)INGMAR(k) (Bergman)
14. IN THE SCRUM (anag)
15. L<ILL>EE
16. NAZ<A/R>E/TH
17. OLD MAN
18. ON <HE>AT
19. OU/CH (Univ. church)
20. OU/T O/F USE
21. PEN/ET/RATED
22. P/LEDGE
23. SENSIBLE
24. T<ACHY>ONS
25. THEREOF (anag)
26. TO-D/O
27. (co)UPON
28,17,5. WHEN THE OLD MAN DIED

176

Jigsaw No. 54 – PERIMETRICAL (Variant)

Perimeter:WHEN (you are) OLD AND GREY*AND FULL OF SLEEP, and nodding by the fire, take down this book, and slowly read ... (W. B. Yeats)

* (This spelling from the MacMillan edition of his *Selected Poems*, 1938; *Oxford Dictionary of Quotations* has 'gray'.)

1. AC<CUS>E	15. MONEYMAKER (anag)
2. A/CROP/HO(me)/BIA(s)	16. NE<I>THER
3. AI/RED/ALE	17. NOUGAT (anag)
4. DASH	18. ODE/A
5. D-IFF<I/CULT>Y	19. ORI<GI(o)>N
6. DR/OM/IO (Comedy of Errors)	20. OVER/STEP
7. EASTER/LIES	21. PE<AT BO>G
8. E/COD	22. RHEUMATICS (anag)
9. FROG/BIT	23. SKY/E
10. HEDGE/HOG	24. S/P/E/Y (strathspey)
11. INS/TALL	25. TEST/ CASE
12. LI<BID>O(n)	26. TRADE-OFF (anag)
13. L<OR>IKE/ET	27. UP<HOLST>ERY
14. LO/WEST	28. WIN/O

177

Jigsaw No. 55 – PERIMETRICAL

Perimeter and 17: THE/RE AR/E NO MIS(rev)/TAKES IN/ LIFE, ONLY(anag)/ LES/SONS

1. A/MEN	15. I/L/LATI<O>N
2. AU/GEAN	16. LAND/-WA<I>TER
3. AYE-AYE	17. LESSONS (lessens)
4. BANK/ROLL	18. LET ME SEE
5. CESURA (anag)	19. LOCI
6. EMB/ALMED (anags)	20. MONTE/BELLO (Belmont)
7. ENCASHME<N>T (anag)	21. NEAR
8. ENTREE	22. OBTRUDE (anag)
9. ES<COR>T (all Fr.)	23. OLD FIRM
10. F<O[L]K> ROCK	24. REV/ELLER(y)
11. FROG	25. RHATANY (hidden)
12. HAW/A/II	26. TO D/ATE
13. HIND/ER/ER	27. WES(rev)/TER ROSS (anag)
14. HONE/Y-<BE>E	28. YO<GIS>M

178

Jigsaw No. 56 – PERIMETRICAL

Perimeter: WITH FRIENDS LIKE THESE WHO NEEDS (anag) [ENEMIES]

1. ALLIANCE
2. DR<EAR>Y
3. ENEMIES
4. ESC<APEMEN>T
5. EV<ERG/L>ADES
6. FLIGHT PATH (fight Plath)
7. GEOTHERMAL (hidden)
8. H<A/RN>ESS
9. HAULIER (anag)
10. HEAR HEAR
11. ICE-AXE (I sax)
12. IN/DAB/A
13. LOG<ICI>AN
14. MEED (rev)
15. MISERE/RE, MISER/ERE
16. NAP/OLI
17. NO/SH
18. NOUS
19. ON/ VI/EW (all rev)
20. OVER/CAST
21. POSTURE (anag)
22. RAN/C<HM>AN
23. REPORT
24. SE<A/PLAN>E
25. SHINER (black-eyed S)
26. SHRINK
27. TRAY
28. WHORES(anag)/ON

Jigsaw No. 57 – PERIMETRICAL (Variant)

Perimeter: (Here will I dwell, for) (Heaven is in these lips) AND ALL IS DROSS THAT IS NOT HELENA (Marlowe, Faustus, scene 14)

1. A/D<V>ENT
2. A<ENE>ID
3. AIRBRUSH (anag) (Harrisbu)
4. A<QUA>RIA
5. AT/HEIST
6. DE/LATI<O>N
7. DOVE/COTE
8. ENTRACTE (anag)
9. HARRIS (3 Men in a Boat)
10,12,18. HEAVE/N IS I/ N <THE/SE L>IPS
11. HOOD/OO
12. See 10
13. K/ERR/I/A
14. KILN (anag)
15. LASS/IE
16. LESS/ON
17. L/ILL/I/BET
18. See 10
19. NESS/US
20. NEUROTIC (anag)
21. QUEEN BEE
22. R<EH>ASH
23. R/OPINES/S
24. SAW/B/ONES
25. SHEARWATER (anag)
26. SHIMEI (anag) (2 Samuel 16.13)
27. THIRTY-CENT (anag) (thentic try)
28. UCCELLO (Italian for 'bird')

Jigsaw No. 58 – PERIMETRICAL (Variant)

Perimeter: WAVERLEY NOVELS; SIR WALTER SCOTT

1. A/BYE	15. L<AM>ENT
2. ACYCLIC (anag)	16. LITT/L/E GO
3. A/EON	17. MACONOCHIE (anag)
4. A/R/TIER	18,8. M<O[LOT]O/V C>OCK/TAIL
5. CAT/GUT(s)	19. PROFI<CIEN>T
6. CAT/O	20. REND/ER/ DOWN
7. CHROMATICS (anag)	21. RETRO<CH/OI>R
8. See 18	22. SHER
9. DITTO/N (Grantchester)	23. TYPESCRIPT (anag)
10. ECHELON (hidden)	24. U<RN>S
11. ELM/O	25. VISA(ge)
12. EX/PO	26. WAND/ER/ER
13. INCREDIBLY (anag)	27. WAX/WORK
14. IR<RIG>ATE	28. WH<ARFED>ALE

Jigsaw No. 59 – PERIMETRICAL (Variant)

Perimeter: PICKWICK PAPERS; CHARLES DICKENS

1. ACCOMPLISH (anag)
2. CHOW/ MEIN
3. CLERGY WIFE (anag)
4. COL/LATI<O>NS
5. CO<OPERATE>D
6. CYST (hidden)
7. EAR<FLA(rev)>PS
8. EMUS (Muse)
9. GUES<T-HOU>S/E
10. HAMNET (Hamlet)
11. H<EN C>O/OP
12. INCA/UT/IOUS
13. (f)INC/HES
14. IR<ON/WOR>K
15. KIN(g)SHIP
16. LENS
17. MOUE (moo)
18. MUM/MER
19. NO/OK
20. PH/LEG/MAT/IC
21. PLEA(sure)
22. ROCK/ALL
23. SA<FA>RI
24. SEASICK (si sic)
25. SEER (Rees)
26. SELF-H(anag)/E/LP
27. SET/A
28. WEALTHIEST (anag)

Jigsaw No. 60 – PERIMETRICAL (Variant)

Perimeter: CRICKET, CROQUET, CURLING, CYCLING

1. AMNIOTIC (anag)	15. INTER/FERES (meddles)
2. BE/D-ROLL	16. IRRESO(anag)/LUTE
3. CALL/AN	17. KEEN
4. CLEMENCEAU (anag)	18. L/ADDERS
5. CO/(a)LUMNA/R	19. L/IN/O(cut)
6. CONNIE (anag)	20. M/I<S/-TEE>Q
7. C/RUMBLE	21. MON<TER>EY
8. ETYMIC (hidden)	22. NON-U/P/LET
9. EX/ACTING	23. RED/O
10. EYR(i)E	24. RU<SH-/HOL>DER
11. FILM CRITIC (anag)	25. SU/FI (rev)
12. FL(ag)/AUNT	26. TI<DEMI>LL
13. GI/VE IN	27. UNS/HOE
14. INGRESSIVE (anag)	28. U/SER

1 ACROSS was first established as 'Subscription Crosswords' by Araucaria in April 1984, to provide puzzles by monthly subscription for readers of *The Guardian* and others who were devotees of his puzzles. He produced four puzzles each month until becoming a 'senior citizen' in 1986, when he decided to reduce his workload a little by joining forces with his youthful protégé John Henderson (Enigmatist of *The Guardian*). The two compilers then produced the puzzles jointly for the next eight years, under Enigmatist's editorship.

In 1991 the format was revamped under the new name of *1 Across* with the addition of a 'guest' puzzle, a prize puzzle, readers' letters and editorial content. In 1994 the editorship passed to the late Michael Rich, and in 2000 to Tom Johnson (Doc of *The Spectator*). The magazine is a source of interesting and ingenious speciality or thematic puzzles by professional and amateur compilers. All puzzles are new and previously unpublished and each issue will usually contain two puzzles by Araucaria.

If you would like details and a free sample copy, please send a C5 sae to Christine Jones at *1 Across*, The Old Chapel, Middleton Tyas, Richmond, North Yorkshire, DL10 6PP.

Chambers publishes a range of books for crosswords of all types, providing the definitive guide to crossword success.

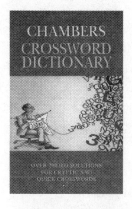

Chambers Crossword Dictionary

The essential reference tool for crossword lovers everywhere. Not only is it easy to use, it is also the most authoritative crossword companion around.

'I love this book ...' *The Herald* Crosswords Editor

'The *Chambers Crossword Dictionary* certainly is a fine book and a safe Christmas present for any crossword fan.' *Amazon*

ISBN: 0550 10006 7
Hardback
Price: £25

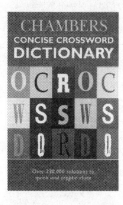

Chambers Concise Crossword Dictionary

Chambers Concise Crossword Dictionary is derived from the top-of-the-range *Chambers Crossword Dictionary*, and is a valuable aid to solving cryptic and quick crossword clues.

ISBN: 0550 12012 2
Paperback
Price: £9.99

Chambers Crossword Manual

Intrigued by the challenges posed by cryptic crosswords but completely flummoxed by the clues and at a loss to know what on earth they mean? *Chambers Crossword Manual* gives you all the help you need to be able to meet the challenges set by the most experienced cruciverbalists working in newspapers today.

ISBN: 0550 12006 8
Paperback
Price: £6.99

Chambers Anagrams

Chambers Anagrams is an ingenious aid to solving anagrams and anagram-based puzzles. An essential handbook for all wordgame enthusiasts, including crossword puzzlers and Scrabble® players, it is indispensable for all wordgames based on rearranging jumbles of letters to form real words.

ISBN: 0550 12005 X
Paperback
Price: £9.99

Chambers Crossword Completer

A unique and innovative arrangement and presentation of words lets the crossword solver complete solutions from the letters already filled in on the grid. With 216,000 words and phrases from 4 to 15 letters long, alphabetically arranged in order of alternate letters, *Chambers Crossword Completer* provides solutions to a wide range of troublesome crossword situations.

ISBN: 0550 12013 0
Paperback
Price: £9.99

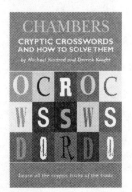

Chambers Cryptic Crosswords and How to Solve Them

Chambers Cryptic Crosswords and How to Solve Them gives all the cryptic tricks of the trade, taught through a series of graded puzzles. Simple summaries of the most commonly encountered clue structures are included, and a two-way crossword glossary explains the language of cryptic crosswords.

ISBN: 0550 10053 9
Paperback
Price: £5.99

Visit our website at www.chambers.co.uk for more wordgame books and online word checkers.